Is God Your Source?

Who Are You Trusting?

by Oral Roberts

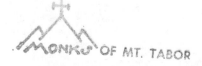

My Dedication

I want to give my daughter-in-law, Lindsay, real credit for helping me put this book together in a way that reflects the way that I really preach. She pressed me to do it. She even went through my sermons. She pulled it out of me and said, "Now, Oral, get down to business and write like you can." And I did.

Thank you, Lindsay!

Oral Roberts

Is God Your Source?

TABLE OF CONTENTS

A Personal Word From Oral Roberts

Friend, my soul is burning with the fire of the truth of what God is revealing to me for His people at this moment concerning making Him our Source.

The magnitude of the importance of His revelation for your life is like fire inside me, filling my being until I can hardly wait to COMMUNICATE it to you. Although I have said before that God is your Source, the powerful anointing on this truth today is like a fresh new wave over me. God's Word to His people is that we must MAKE GOD OUR SOURCE — and the time to make God our Source is NOW. God's people are *not* to live in poverty physically, spiritually, or financially. God is in *your* now and *you* are in God's now.

One of the tactics of the devil is to try to cut God's people off from their Source. Without that divine, miraculous supply from God as their Source, His people are robbed of their faith, their hope, and all things necessary to live life as God intended. God has already provided everything we need for our lives, and He is serious about our having our needs met.

We must learn the biblical way to get our needs met, and that is by faith in God our Source. God wanted us to realize that *the just shall live by faith* so much that He put it in His Word in four places: *Habakkuk 2:4, Romans 1:17, Galatians 3:11, and Hebrews 10:38*. He said we must live by faith DAILY, and not merely use it when we need a quick solution to an immediate problem. God wants us, as His children, to live every day of our lives "by faith."

In *I Chronicles 12:32* we read about the men of Issachar, men who *"had understanding of the times, to know what Israel ought to do.*" You see, in every generation, God provides men and women of God (the prophets, apostles, evangelists, pastors, and teachers) who are tuned in to Him as He speaks. Then they tell what they have heard from God to His people so they might know *"what they ought to do."* In the world we live in today, I don't know where we as Christians would be without a word from God. How could we know what God wants us to do?

I love God's Word. I praise God for <u>THE</u> Word, for the Bible says in *Matthew 24:35, "Heaven and earth shall pass away but my words shall not pass away."* And, I praise God for the **Rhema Word** — the word by revelation knowledge that God reveals to the Body of Christ through people like His anointed prophets.

Friend, it all comes down to one question — *do you want to live life under the devil's domination, or turn to God as the Source of your total life-giving supply?* I pray that by the time you finish this book you will have reached up to Heaven with your faith and touched God, who is a good God and the Source of everything good for your life. Don't miss one word of the testimonies throughout this book of people like you and me who were changed in their total beings when they made <u>God their Source</u> of total supply.

DON'T MISS THESE WORDS

Hear these words with the very **EARS OF YOUR HEART AND SOUL** — don't just read them as idle lines on paper. Let these words that I have for you register in the core of your innermost being. Command your spirit man, not your natural man, to hear these words, and then respond to them with the full force of your **FAITH**. Hear me, Oral Roberts, when I say, "**I AM ALIVE** today because I made God the Source of my spiritual, physical, and financial supply, the Source of my total healing."

In *II Chronicles 20:20*, God established the importance of His prophets when He said, *"Believe in the Lord your God, so shall you be established; believe his prophets, so shall you prosper."*

When a prophet of God has a word from God we **MUST** listen, but not just listen, we must <u>believe</u> in order to prosper according to *II Chronicles*. How does Oral Roberts minister as a prophet of God? I have no doubt in my heart that God speaks to me in the spirit of a prophet, and when He speaks and I obey, miracles happen.

Friend, God has spoken to me again about making Him the Source of our total supply. I believe as we obey God we will be established, and as we believe His prophets we will prosper and miracles will be our portion in Jesus' Name!

If I could stand in your living room with you right now, I would put my face right into yours, place my hands on your shoulders, and with every fiber of my being I would pray for you to MAKE GOD YOUR SOURCE.

Make Him your **PHYSICAL SOURCE.**
Make Him your **FINANCIAL SOURCE.**
    And, above ALL,
Make Him your **SPIRITUAL SOURCE.**

THE SOURCE OF YOUR TOTAL SUPPLY.

When the Apostle Paul said in *Philippians 4:19,* *"But my God shall supply ALL YOUR NEED according to his riches in glory by Christ Jesus,"* he meant ALL. He said ALL your needs and he meant exactly that — ALL your needs. What does that mean for your life right now, today?

It means that:

God can supply enough to meet all your physical needs.

God can supply enough to meet all of your financial needs.

God can supply enough to meet all of your spiritual needs . . . when you make Him THE SOURCE OF YOUR TOTAL SUPPLY.

I. GOD IS THE SOURCE OF YOUR PHYSICAL SUPPLY

1. THE LETTER THAT SHOOK MY SOUL

2. THE MIRACLE THAT SHOOK MY SOUL

3. THE GOD WHO SHOOK MY SOUL

4. THE SCRIPTURE THAT SHOOK MY SOUL

5. THE CHILDREN WHO SHOOK MY SOUL
   Jacob Garrison
   Beau Van Geffen
   Joshua Wilson

CHAPTER 1

THE LETTER THAT SHOOK MY SOUL

I received a testimony from a longtime Partner who was dramatically healed of cancer as a result of learning God is the Source of her PHYSICAL supply.

This Partner was in her mid-thirties when she lost her beloved husband to cancer. She had three young children and was facing a terrible business situation as a result of her husband's death. Immediately following his death, she personally began to experience a series of illnesses, weight loss, and other serious problems. Things went from bad to worse.

Then, just as the devil would have it, she received the shocking news that cancer had now struck her own body. But, as the Lord would have it, she had just written for my new (at the time) book, **Three Most Important Steps to Your Better Health and Miracle Living.**

The first part of the book dealt with making God your Source. She said this hit her soul like lightning and she released her faith to God for her healing in a way like never before. I want to share her letter with you so you can begin to release your faith for miracles to come in your own life. Don't miss <u>one</u> word — not

<u>one</u> *word — of her letter as you read it, for I believe the rest of her story will hit home in a very unusual way.*

Dear Brother Oral,

In November 1976, I had a surgery for a hys- terectomy. Before that surgery I had had a routine chest X-ray and the doctor discovered a spot on my right lung that would require more surgery as soon as I recovered from the hysterectomy. After the first operation, I was sent to the hospital every week for an X-ray of my lungs.

I have been a Partner of your ministry for many years and I always watch your Sunday television program. During the TV program one morning, you offered your new book, *Three Most Important Steps to Your Better Health and Miracle Living.* You said you would send it free and postpaid. I wrote and requested a book. The day I received my book I started to read it and claim every promise and Scripture God gave you in the book. I was so encouraged by the book that I got more copies, and each time I went to the hospital for an X-ray, I took several books with me and left them in the sitting rooms so that others could receive hope as I had.

My physician sent me to a thoracic specialist and it seemed that each time they would try to schedule me for surgery for the spot on my lung, something would come up and I would have to reschedule. One afternoon as I was sitting in the X-ray room, I was reading your book when I felt a warm hand on my body in the exact area where the spot was. I looked around to see who had touched me, but found there was no one else in the room. I felt a warm heat all over the area where I had been touched. Right then, I knew beyond a shadow of a doubt that God had touched me. My doctor suggested that we should just <u>watch</u> the spot. He didn't feel we should do surgery at this time, but I knew God had healed me. That was 14-1/2 years ago. Today I'm alive and well and praising God for it!

Thank you, Brother Oral, for being an obedient, faithful servant of God.

Your Partner,
Patricia Salem

Friend, this letter shook me to my core for two reasons.

First, because this precious woman got a miracle when she touched God, her Source, with her faith. That life-saving healing miracle was 14-1/2 years ago, and today Mrs. Salem is an active woman, enjoying her many grandchildren.

Second, after I read this letter and looked at the signature, I realized that it was from my daughter-in-law's (Lindsay's) own mother. Patricia and her husband, Harry Salem, were longtime Partners from Flint, Michigan. After Mr. Salem's homegoing, their family moved to Florida. Lindsay graduated from college and came to ORU to attend law school. She and Richard met, fell in love, were married and have a beautiful family here as a part of this ministry. I shake in my soul to see the reality of the healing power of Jesus Christ hit so close to home in my own family. And I know that same power is available to you and your loved ones as you make God the Source of miracles for your physical needs.

*My dear friend, I can't say it strongly enough —
God is a healing God when we make Him the
Source of our <u>PHYSICAL</u> <u>SUPPLY.</u>*

Make Him your **PHYSICAL SOURCE.**
Make Him your **FINANCIAL SOURCE.**
    And, above ALL,
Make Him your **SPIRITUAL SOURCE.**

THE SOURCE OF YOUR TOTAL SUPPLY.

NOTE: To receive your copy of *Three Most Important Steps to
Your Better Health and Miracle Living,* send in the request
form in the back of this book.

CHAPTER 2

THE MIRACLE THAT SHOOK MY SOUL

"Tell Oral Roberts I have lung cancer and I'm here for prayer."

This note for prayer was handed to me while I was standing outside in the heat of one of Oklahoma's blistering summers. God had placed it on my heart to write my Partners and tell them to send in a letter or an item representing their greatest needs. He also had instructed me to have a "tent service" — a healing service representative of the tent cathedral crusades that signatured my ministry for so many years. We did just what God instructed.

As I listened to God as my Source and obeyed His words, thousands of letters and phone calls flooded in to our ministry from our Partners with requests for prayer for their needs. We pitched a tent on the campus of Oral Roberts University by the Prayer Tower, the centerpiece of our campus where prayer goes up 24 hours a day, 7 days a week. Now the media thought we were crazy and some of them poked fun at our obedience to God, but there was a certain woman who didn't laugh at our obedience, but acted in faith and got a miracle because of it.

This woman had received my letter at her home in Alabama, and responded back with her prayer request. But then something happened — God instructed her to get in her car, drive to Tulsa to

SEE ORAL ROBERTS. As God would have it, and as God ORDERED her steps (the steps of the righteous are ordered of God, see Psalm 37:23), she obeyed orders and received her miracle! Read Janice's testimony as she gave it on our Sunday "Miracles Now" TV program.

I never expected to be a part of the actual tent service that Oral told us about in his letter, because his letter did not state a time that we were to be there. The letter just said that on that particular day Richard and Oral Roberts would be praying over all the needs that had been sent in, and that they were digging a hole to plant those needs in the ground under the shadow of the Prayer Tower. I never dreamed my husband and I would ever have a part in the service, we went because we felt in our spirit we were to go.

At the tent service, Oral and Richard were getting ready to pray over the thousands of needs written on prayer sheets that had been put into the hole in the ground. But right before they prayed, Oral stopped and asked, "Where's the lady who drove out here from Alabama?" My mouth must have dropped open because I just couldn't believe it — they were calling for me. I had not spoken to them, I had just handed them a note with my request for prayer for lung cancer. I answered, "Here I am." They had me go up in front of everybody, and then they laid hands on me as a point of contact while they prayed for me.

After they prayed, strength was restored instantly to me right in that service. When I came to Tulsa I had been too weak to walk ten feet without having to hold onto my husband, and I would almost faint. Now, after prayer, I jumped up as high as I could jump, and then I ran as long and as fast as I could — all the way down that hill to other buildings on the ORU campus and then back again to where the service was going on. I was not tired or exhausted, I was just totally healed. Everything about me was restored back to normal. I just rejoiced in the Lord because I had been instantly restored. I know that a lot of people get healed and they get better over time, but I didn't just get better — I got restored instantly! I not only got a miracle of healing — I was made whole instantly from that disease.

After his prayer, Oral said to me, "I want you to go home, call and make an appointment with the doctors who diagnosed the cancer, have X-rays and follow-up tests made, and let them tell you that you are healed."

I told him, "Oral Roberts, that appointment was made before I even came to Tulsa, Oklahoma. That appointment is set. I already made the appointment that is going to tell me that I am well."

I returned home, went back to the doctors and they made the X-rays. While my husband and I were waiting for the results, the doctor came in carrying the X-ray, and put it up on a little dark board. Before he flipped the light on, I said, "You've got something that you're not going to believe when you flip that light on." He turned around and said, "What?" I said, "I've been healed. God healed me. When you flip that light on, you're going to see. God healed me."

So he looked at the X-ray, and he looked at the X-ray, and he looked some more at the X-ray. Then I said, "Well, what do you think?" He said, "There is no other explanation. I have to go along with the fact that God has healed you!" Then he asked, "Would you mind if I run an oxygen level test on you?" I said, "I don't mind." I had had the test run before when I could hardly breathe. So they hooked the wires to me, plugged the machine in and turned it on. I could see the digital readout on the machine, and when they plugged it in and flipped it on, it read 97, 98, 99, 100. And it just sat right there on 100 — perfectly normal.

Then the doctor said, "Would you come back in three months and let us make some more X-rays to look at?" I said, "I'll come back whenever you say come back, because I know I'm healed and the cancer is never coming back."

I went back in December and had follow-up X-rays made, and I went back again in March. When I went back a third time in June, the X-rays were still clear and there was still no sign of cancer. God gave my life back to me through prayer.

Notice three things here:
#1 — Janice was familiar with hearing God's Word, so when He told her to get in the car and go to Tulsa, it didn't sound strange to her. We must be familiar with God and His Word so when He speaks, we listen.

#2 — She did something beyond just hearing God's Word. Once she heard it, she acted on it. James 2:26 says, "Faith without works is dead." Janice could have chosen to let her faith and her life fall apart at the news of having cancer. But instead, she put her faith into action and did what God said

to do when He said to do it.

#3 — She was persistent. She did not let circumstances get in her way. She acted on God's Word and did not settle for less than a miracle. And when she activated her persistent faith with the Word of God and her own works, she made a point of contact for the releasing of her own faith and a miracle was her portion as she made God the Source of her total supply.

*You can do these three things, too, just as Janice did: (1) Know God's Word, (2) Obey God's Word, and (3) Be persistent! Then believe for your **MIRACLE HEALING DELIVERANCE!***

Make Him your **PHYSICAL SOURCE.**
Make Him your **FINANCIAL SOURCE.**
 And, above ALL,
Make Him your **SPIRITUAL SOURCE.**

THE SOURCE OF YOUR TOTAL SUPPLY.

CHAPTER 3

THE GOD WHO SHOOK MY SOUL

I've told the story of my healing testimony over and over again, and I have for so many years felt like putting that part of my life behind me and moving forward into the more recent miracles I've experienced. Yet, God won't let me get away from sharing the story of my life and my miraculous healing from tuberculosis. I believe that's because He realizes the powerful impact my testimony will have in helping people like you learn to make God your Source!

I was born Granville Oral Roberts, in Bebee, Oklahoma (a wide spot in the road), the son of Ellis and Claudius Priscilla Roberts. Mamma and Papa were sharecroppers. Being a sharecropper means you do all the work and the man who owns the land gets most all the money. We were so poor, the poor folks called us poor. We did not live on the back side of the world, but we could see it from our back porch.

Being a stutterer with the name "Oral," which means "spoken word," caused some problems for me growing up. When I tried to recite in front of my classmates or even talk to my friends, the words would stick in my mouth. My stammering and stuttering made me the laughingstock of the whole school.

"Talk for us, Oral!" the kids would taunt.

"He can't talk," they laughed, "he can't even say his name."

I reacted angrily to their making fun of me. And I also directed my anger at myself for stuttering. My life was a cycle of frustration.

The religious convictions that Mamma and Papa held did not make my life any easier at that time. Papa had become a part-time preacher in that rural section of Oklahoma, and ministered mostly among other poor people. He had come from a long line of Methodists, but a move of the Holy Spirit was beginning to awaken people to more of the personal presence and power of Jesus. "Pentecostal" power began to fall and my parents embraced it, including healing by faith. To make matters worse for me, Mamma and Papa kept telling everybody I was going to be a preacher. That confused me because I knew when I tried to talk, I became like I was tongue-tied.

One afternoon while playing with some boys who began to taunt me about my stammering tongue, my frustration reached the boiling point. In utter despair, I ran home and burst into the kitchen where Mamma was. Tears were streaming down my face as I cried out my hurt to her.

Mamma, sitting in an old cane-bottomed chair we had in the kitchen, pulled me close to her and said to me, "Oral, I made a covenant with God for your life. I gave you to Him before you were born. One day you will preach the Gospel."

By that time we were both crying. I looked up at Mamma and asked, "M-m-m-mamma, h-h-how c-c-can I-I p-p-preach? I-I-I c-c-can't even t-t-t-talk!"

She framed my face with the hardworking hands of an Oklahoma sharecropper's wife and answered, "Son, you are going to preach because God is going to heal you." She would not give up. To everyone else, the idea of stammering, stuttering Oral Roberts ever becoming a preacher was silly, but not to Mamma Roberts.

Leaving Home to Make My Future

As I grew into my teens I began to drift away from God and the Methodist church of which I was a member. Many nights, as I lay in bed listening to my parents' prayers for my brothers, Elmer and Vaden, and my sister, Jewel, and me, I felt their love as though it was coming right through the walls. But satan fought me day  and night. I rebelled hard against God and the teachings of the church and my parents. I rebelled against the abject poverty in which we lived. I was tired of living in a two-room shack, never having enough clothes, never having enough to eat, my shoes having holes in them, and my feeling that I was being looked down on by just about everybody in the community.

In the mornings when I went out to feed the chickens and milk the cows, I looked down the dusty farm road, beyond the rolling Oklahoma hills and wondered just what lay in store for me. I had begun to dream of becoming a lawyer someday. I had to do something to get away. Anything, I thought, would be better than this.

At night, the heat of the summer was unbearable. There was no such thing as an air conditioner. We didn't even own a fan. As I lay on my bed trying to sleep, I could feel the sweat running down the side of my face; occasionally I could hear the whine of a mosquito and feel its sharp bite. As I lay there looking out the window at the twinkling stars, I made a decision . . . I was leaving home; I would tell Mamma and Papa in the morning.

I had my speech all planned. I was going to box up my few belongings and bravely walk in and tell them, "I am going out into the world and make it on my own. I am going to walk through that door and down the dusty road of life. I don't know where I am going or exactly what I am going to do, but don't worry, I'll make it. I am a man now. I have been wanting to leave for some time, but last night I made up my mind. Today is the day, my day to start toward the dream of a new life." In my mind I could see Mamma and Papa being hurt, but finally wishing me well and sending me off with best wishes.

My going-away speech was not as flowery as I planned, and Mamma and Papa did not react the way I had imagined they would. They were hurt all right. I could see the hurt in Papa's eyes. But he didn't have any well-wishes for me.

"Oral," he said, "if you run away I'll send the police after you. They will find you and bring you back."

Angry, I struck back, "It won't do any good, Papa, I'll just run away again."

Mamma came over to me. I was getting tall, already over six feet. Mamma, who was only five feet tall, pulled me down to her, put her hands on my shoulders, looked full into my face and said, "Oral, you can't outrun my prayers. I know Papa and I don't have anything to offer you except love, a home, and raising you right. I won't try to stand in your way because I know you have made up your mind to leave and I can't stop you. But wherever you go, my prayers will be there for you. I will pray until God sends you back."

I walked across the room, pushed that old screen door open, and let it slam behind me. The old, gray, faded planks squeaked as I stepped off the front porch into the yard. I turned around and saw Papa and Mamma looking at me through the screen door with all the love and compassion a parent could feel for their child. Mamma's tears were still wet on my cheeks where she had kissed me.

Nothing Could Stop Me

As I walked down the road toward my long-awaited freedom, the very hills seemed to echo what Mamma told me.  "Oral, you'll never outrun my prayers. I will pray until God sends you home." This thing was not proceeding exactly like I thought it was going to. But I was determined and kept walking. It was the enemy of my soul who made me run from Papa's preaching and Mamma's prayers. I understand the battles of the young people of today. I know how they feel "turned-off" by the church, the establishment, their parents, and society. As a teenager I felt all those same nagging, emotional pains they feel.

At that time we were living in Ada, Oklahoma, the county seat of Pontotoc County where I had been born. I went to Atoka, Oklahoma, where I secured a room with a judge's family. After dinner each evening I was allowed to study the judge's law books. I went through these books with all the hunger of a young animal searching for food. I dreamed in my mind, while clutching those law books in my hand, of someday becoming a lawyer and then going on to become the governor of the state of Oklahoma.

To support myself I followed a very demanding schedule. I served as a handyman at the home of the judge. I took a job at a grocery store on Saturdays, threw a paper route, and wrote a column and served as a reporter for my hometown newspaper, *The Ada Evening News*.

I arose each morning at four o'clock and built the fires. I went to bed around midnight after I finished the day's classes, practiced basketball, threw my paper route, wrote my column, and maybe even had a date. In school I carried a full load, too. I loved to study and I was an A student.

When I left Mamma and Papa's home and started down that dusty road, I was determined to make something of myself. I was working very hard at doing just that. In spite of my stuttering, I was elected president of my class and made the starting lineup on the basketball team.

But I was pushing myself beyond my physical capabilities. Besides being born a stutterer, I was also born with very weak lungs. I began having small pains in my chest and waking up at night in deep sweats. I started tiring easily, and many times after a basketball game it felt as if my lungs were going to explode. Every now and then I spat up blood when I coughed, but I thought nothing of it. I was excited by what was going on, fascinated by life, and getting more confident every day. I saw nothing but my future before me and nothing could stop me.

My Dreams and Hopes Destroyed

My whole world came crashing down around me one night in the final game of the southeastern Oklahoma basketball tournament. The ball was passed to me. I moved around the man guarding me and dribbled down the court. The crowd was on its feet cheering me on. The roar was deafening as I dribbled across the floor and drove in for a lay-up as hard and fast as I could.

Suddenly everything began to fade before my eyes. I stumbled and collapsed on the gymnasium floor. Blood began running out of my mouth, I lost consciousness briefly and began hemorrhaging with every breath. My coach, Mr. Herman Hamilton, rushed over to me and soon he and some of the players and fans carried me out to his car and laid me on the back seat. "Oral," he said, "I'm taking you home."

I was so afraid as I lay in Coach Hamilton's car looking out into the night. All my hopes, my dreams for the future, my ambitions were dashed to pieces in minutes. I did not know what was wrong, but I knew whatever it was, it was bad. I also knew I was heading back to poverty, back to a religious home I had never accepted, and back to my parents' strict discipline. It crushed me inside.

When we pulled up in Mamma and Papa's front yard, Coach Hamilton went up to the front door and knocked.

"Reverend Roberts?" I heard him say. (By this time Papa was pastoring a small church.)

"Yes," my father answered, "is something wrong?"

Coach Hamilton said, "Reverend Roberts, I've brought your son home. Can you help me carry him in?"

When Mamma saw Papa and my coach carrying me in, she cried, "Oh God! I didn't know he would come home like this!"

They carried me into the bedroom and put me into bed. Although most Pentecostals at that time believed strongly in divine healing and had very little to do with doctors or the medical professions, my dad was an exception. The doctors were called in and began making their examinations. The pain in my lungs was terrible. At night I coughed and hemorrhaged so much that eventually the wallpaper beside my bed had to be removed and new wallpaper put on.

Death Stared Me in the Face

One day after the doctor had examined me and left, Papa came into my room. Tears welled up in his eyes as he tried to speak to me.

I said, "Papa, what's wrong?"

He said, "Son, you are going to be all right."

"Well," I said, "if I'm going to be all right, why are you crying?"

Papa replied, "You're going to be all right, son."

I knew something dreadful was wrong. I said, "Papa, tell me the truth. What is wrong with me? Why do my lungs hurt? Why do I cough up blood?

Why do I not want to eat anymore?"

I could not believe it, but he assured me it was true. I had tuberculosis and was to be sent to the state tubercular sanitorium at Talihina, in the mountains of eastern Oklahoma.

That was 1935. In those days there was no penicillin or what are called "miracle drugs," and to have tuberculosis at age 17 was a much greater threat than it would be today. Relatives of mine had died with tuberculosis. My oldest sister, Velma, had died at 19 with pneumonia. The stark reality of death was staring me in the face.

When my brother Vaden was told, he came in crying and flung himself across the bed, asking God to let him have the disease instead of me. I finally pushed him off me and reached over to the nightstand where my medicine was. I picked up the medicine and said, "Here, Papa, take this away from me."

"What do you mean, Oral?" Papa asked.

I said, "Papa, if there is no cure for tuberculosis and I am going to die, then this medicine isn't going to do any good." I was giving up!

Mamma came into my room, took my hand, and started talking to me. I finally stopped her by saying, "Mamma, what did your daddy die of?"

She looked down at me, but she would not answer.

Again I said, "Mamma, answer me. What did your daddy die of?"

Finally, she answered, "He died of tuberculosis!"

Can you imagine how I felt? This only confirmed my fears that I, too, was going to die. I lay there day after day questioning why this should happen to me. What had I done to deserve this?

Mamma Would Not Give Up

Mamma, however, was convinced that God was going to heal me, and she urged my father to write everyone we knew to pray and believe God for my healing. She just would not give up. Sometimes entire groups of these friends would come to stay with us a day or two to pray for me. It all seemed like a dream. I looked at them through eyes that really didn't see, and I listened to them through ears that really didn't hear.

I talked often with my mother about my future, of being a lawyer. She would smooth my pillow, put her hand on me or lean over and kiss my brow, and say, "We'll see, son, we'll see."

Each time I looked into her face, I remembered the many times she had held me close and told me that someday I would be a preacher. Then I began to grow bitter that my lungs felt like they were bursting inside, that I had fever nearly all the time, and that when I tried to stand and walk I was so weak that I stumbled and fell and had to have Mamma and Papa pick me up and put me back on the bed.

So he could be with me all the time, Papa accepted an appointment at a smaller church in Stratford, Oklahoma, 18 miles to the west of Ada. People by the dozens came and went from our house. They came to see the preacher's boy who lay dying with tuberculosis at such a tender age. Some came to pray, some just came to show sympathy.

When Papa and Mr. Hamilton, the basketball coach, had put me into bed I weighed 165 pounds and had a 6-foot 1-1/2 inch frame. After lying bedfast for 163 days my weight dropped to 120 pounds. My friends could no longer recognize me. In fact, when they came to visit me, they could hardly stand to look at me: I had bedsores from lying in bed so long.

Food tasted like wood to me. Sharp pains that went clear through to my shoulder blades were constantly in my chest now. Night sweats were also constant, and the bloody, hacking cough was always there. I began to curse the day I was born. I was giving up.

I had a lot of medicine: some prescribed by doctors, and some home remedies prescribed by well-meaning friends.

Prayers were said over me constantly, and from time to time predictions were made that for me the end was near. Except for the suffering in my body, I lived in a state of unreality. My mind was in a shadow and I felt very far away from normal life.

I Thought I Would Die, But I Wanted to Live

I didn't respond to my parents' wishes to pray or to let Christ become more real to me. A stupor engulfed me, and at last, it was as though I didn't see or hear anyone. I refused to take any more medicine, saying, "If I'm going to die anyway, why take that bitter-tasting stuff?"

My pastor from my church came to visit and pray with me. (I had kept my membership in a church of a different denomination even though my father had become a Pentecostal Holiness minister. Most of my young friends were from this church I had joined.) Now, as my pastor started to leave, he said, "Oral, you've just got to be patient."

I had never been patient, even when I was well, and now I was certainly not interested in patiently waiting to die. Brother, I thought, if this is all the Lord has to offer, I don't want Him.

My parents' religion was equally repelling.

Folks would gather in my parents' home and discuss my case. I could hear them talk from where I lay dying. On and on they would go with their opinions about why I was sick. They would come into my room, pray for me and say, "Oral, God loves you. Let Him have your life." But when they went into the other room, their stories seemed to change. They all seemed to agree on one thing: God had stricken me with this killing disease. I was so confused. I could not figure out why God, if He loved me, would do such a thing to me. Why would He want me struck down like this?

These people would talk to me about going to Heaven. They found it very difficult to appreciate my response: "I'm not interested in dying and going to Heaven, nor am I interested in dying and going to hell. I am interested in living and getting well."

One Wednesday evening Papa sent word to one of his deacons to take charge of that evening's service. I knew something was going on. I said to Papa, "Are you not going to church tonight?"

"No," Papa replied, "I am not going to church. Oral, I am not giving up on you. I am going to get on my knees and pray until I hear from Heaven."

Now that I have children of my own, I can appreciate Papa's grim determination not to let the devil kill his baby boy. Papa knelt at the foot of my bed and leaned across it. He's with Jesus now, after having lived 87 years, but I can still hear him praying for me and see him on his knees at the end of my bed. I don't ever remember Papa praying as hard as he prayed that night. When he raised his head from my bed, the front of his shirt was drenched with his tears.

The Beginning of a Miracle

What happened next was the beginning of a series of events that led to my healing and my call into the ministry of healing. Suddenly, while Papa had his hands raised and his face looking upward, my eyes blinked wide open in total amazement, my heart beat faster, my mouth gaped — in place of my father's face was the face of the Lord Jesus Christ. I can't tell you what went racing through my mind, but I can tell you that hope surged in my heart.

Not too long after, the second dramatic event took place in the grocery store while Mamma was shopping. As she walked down the aisle of the market picking up a few things for us to eat, she began to weep. By the time she got to the cash register, tears were dripping off her tired face. As she fumbled, trying to open her little change purse, the grocer said, "Mrs. Roberts, I can't help but notice your tears. Why are you crying? Did Oral die?"

"No, sir," Mamma said, "these are not tears of sorrow, they are tears of joy. God just gave me the assurance Oral is going to be healed! My son is going to get a miracle from the Lord Jesus!" The grocer had given up. He had expected me to die at any time and he figured it had finally happened. But Mamma never did give up! I don't think I have ever seen a woman with more determination than my mother. She had the look of eagles in her eyes. She never doubted that God would keep the covenant she made with Him before my birth.

The third thing which stirred me inwardly happened through my sister Jewel. Jewel lived in Ada, 18 miles away. One afternoon she had an irresistible urge to come to our house. When she got there she walked straight into my room, looked down into my face, and preached the most dynamic faith sermon I have heard to this very day. I say that because she preached it straight to me. It wasn't very long. In fact, it only contained seven words. But to me, those words were the greatest I had ever heard. Now you must remember, sermons had not reached me! Beautiful hymns had not reached me! The church people had not reached me! What Jewel said shook me from the center of my being to the circumference. She said, **"Oral, God is going to heal you."** Through those seven words Jesus was identified to me, He was made real to me. He became part of my life, my future, my very existence. He knew I existed. I was a person to Him, a human being worth saving. It was at that moment I realized Jesus was concerned about me!

Even though I was born with a stuttering, stammering tongue, He cared about me! Even though I had run away from home, He cared about me! Even though I had turned my back on Him and my parents and had forsaken their teachings, He cared about me! He had known about me all the time and He was going to heal me! Thank God that Jewel and the rest of my family never gave up on me. THEY HELD ON TO GOD FOR ME, WHEN I COULD NOT HOLD ON FOR MYSELF.

One day, not long after Jewel had spoken those seven words of deliverance to me, I was laying in my bedroom, still very sick. The sun was just setting on the hills behind our house when I heard the sound of a car. I listened as the car pulled up into our driveway. The brakes gave a loud squeak and the engine stopped. The door slammed shut and footsteps began approaching our porch. I heard the thump . . . thump . . . thump of heavy shoes walking across the porch and the screen door creaking open. Slam! The door shut and the steps neared my room, and around the door, into my room stepped my oldest brother Elmer.

Elmer said to me, "Oral, get up and get dressed!"

"Elmer," I said, "I can't get up. I am too weak."

He said, "I'll help you get up."

Mamma and Papa, who were in the other room, heard the voices and came in. "Why, Elmer," Papa said, "what are you doing here?"

"I have come to get Oral. There is a tent meetin' over in Ada, and the preacher is praying for sick people and they're gettin' healed. Ory [Elmer's wife: her name was Ora, but country folks pronounced it Ory] took me down to the meetin' and I saw people I knew gettin' healed. Oral, I saw it with my own eyes."

I couldn't figure out what had happened to Elmer. I was only about five years old when he had married and moved away, so I didn't know him real well, but I knew he wasn't any more religious than I was. Something had definitely happened to make Elmer get this excited about a revival meeting.

He kept on telling me what he had seen on the previous night of the revival. "Oral," he said, "this preacher prays for everything. After he prays, people testify that they feel better. He preaches different than what we've heard. He tells all about faith and how God can heal people of all kinds of sickness. Last night while I was sittin' there watchin' all those people get healed, I told Ory I was goin' to bring you and let you get healed, too. Now get dressed!"

This announcement that Elmer made didn't seem to surprise Mamma too much. "Well," she said, "I knew God was going to heal him." Like I said, Mamma just did not give up.

"Where did you get that car?" Papa asked.

"I borrowed it!" Elmer said. "And I took the last 35¢ I had to buy gas."

Elmer worked at the flour mill. He made about $10 per week, and that 35¢ was all he had left until payday. (Gasoline was 14¢ a gallon at that time.)

"Well, let's get him dressed and get him down there," Papa said.

My Appointment With Destiny

They all helped me get out of bed and started dressing me. I had only one suit. I had bought that one when I weighed 165 pounds. When they put my clothes on me, the suit literally hung on my body. I wrapped it around me. They put my shoes on me and Elmer carried me, mattress and all, and put me in the back seat of that borrowed car. We couldn't afford an ambulance to take me to the meeting.

As Elmer stepped off the porch with me in his arms, I saw determination in his eyes — determination to get his baby brother some help . . . even if it meant spending his last 35¢ for gas! The thought ran through my mind then, "Elmer really loves me." Elmer hadn't given up. It felt so good to have him hold my sick body with the love and compassion he was showing toward me. It felt good just to realize my family had not given up!

Elmer, Mamma, and Papa got into the front seat after putting me in the back seat. Down the road we went, that old car bouncing in the ruts and the dust flying. Just a few months before, I had gone down the same road toward what I thought was my freedom. This time — though I didn't know it then — **I was going down the road toward my personal appointment with destiny!**

As I rode along, listening to my family's conversation and the rattle of the gravel hitting on the bottom of the car, the sound of the gravel, the conversation, and the roar of the motor began to fade away. Those sounds were replaced with another kind of sound, gradually increasing in volume, coming from within me! My entire being was filled with that sound! Suddenly, from within, the voice of God began to speak! My whole body seemed to fill up with His voice, speaking not only in me but to me, **"Son, I am going to heal you, and you are to take My healing power to your generation."**

I didn't understand all God was saying to me, but it helped me endure the long ride to the tent revival in Ada. I was so sore in my body that each bump the car hit sent pain racing through me. When we arrived, the tent was already overflowing. In a special section, a multitude of sick people lay on cots, sat in wheelchairs, sat holding crutches and canes. Mothers held their sick babies, some even had nightclothes on.

Papa got out of the car first. He went inside and found an empty rocking chair with pillows on both sides. They carried me in and sat me down in that chair. The service began!

Loose Him . . . In the Name of Jesus!

Elmer was right! This church service was different than the ones we were used to. There was something "electric" in the air. In later years, of course, I would come to know this feeling as the divine presence of the Holy Spirit. The preacher's words were charged with this feeling; his eyes flashed with authority as he spoke the miraculous Name of Jesus Christ of Nazareth.

Up to that point, my family had held on for my

healing. Now I was holding on. I did not know one man could preach as long as that preacher did. I could hardly wait for him to get to the part of the service where he prayed for the sick. Finally, he got around to that! He prayed for everybody in the tent! Everybody, that is, but me! It was getting close to midnight. I thought he would never pray for me, but I wasn't doubting God. He had spoken to me on the way to this very service. Whether this preacher prayed for me or not, I believed I was going to get healed.

Just when I thought he wasn't going to get to me to pray, he walked over to me. He looked me straight in the eye. Then he prayed, "YOU FOUL, TORMENTING DISEASE, I COMMAND YOU, IN THE NAME OF JESUS CHRIST OF NAZARETH, COME OUT OF THIS BOY'S LUNGS. LOOSE HIM AND LET HIM GO!"

I had never heard a prayer like that. I had never felt such authority from a man. The only prayers I had heard for my healing began, "Lord, if it be Thy will. . . ." This man wasn't playing around. He meant business!

While I listened to him praying I felt something. It started at the bottom of my feet and moved up my legs. Soon it was flooding my chest and my whole body. I felt strength flowing into my weakened, diseased body. I had learned to breathe from the top of my lungs because when I took deep breaths I hemorrhaged badly. But now, as the healing Spirit of the Lord surged through my body, I began taking deep breaths! I was breathing to the bottom of my lungs! This was more than I could comprehend. All at once I leaped up and shouted to the top of my voice, "I am healed! God has healed me!" I raced back and forth on the platform and just kept shouting as loudly as I could, "I am healed! I am healed! I am healed!"

When I finally settled down, which took a little while because the Roberts family was having their own personal revival, the preacher came over to me smiling. He took hold of my arm and said, "Son, tell the people what the Lord has just done for you."

All of my life I had been a stutterer. I would freeze on the spot when faced by crowds. At school if I had to give an oral book report in front of the class, I would stutter so badly that I would sometimes have to sit down from embarrassment. But that night, when I took the microphone from his hands, I spoke to that crowd like it was my revival. My tongue was loose! I could talk! I could breathe all the way down without coughing or hemorrhaging. I walked up and down the platform telling the people, over the microphone, exactly what Jesus of Nazareth had done for me.

All the way home that night, my thoughts kept going back to when Mamma held me in her arms as a stuttering child chased home by taunting classmates and told me, "Son, you are going to preach the Gospel. Jesus is going to heal you."

Words cannot express how happy I was that Mamma didn't give up . . . Papa didn't give up . . . Elmer didn't give up . . . Jewel didn't give up . . . Vaden didn't give up . . . and I didn't give up! Months of holding on to Mamma's covenant with God were rewarded that spring night.

Was I Really Healed?

I was healed completely of tuberculosis in that meeting. However, it took me several weeks to get my strength back. During that time, the enemy confronted me again with giving up. This time, *my* faith was challenged to give up on my healing.

One afternoon I sat outside our little house, leaning up against the wall. I was confused about whether or not I had really gotten healed. I could not understand why, if I was healed, I did not get all my strength back. About that time Mamma walked around the corner of the house. She came over to me and said, "Oral, you're wondering if you really did get healed, aren't you?"

"Mamma," I said softly, "I'm awfully weak and tired. What if I didn't get healed?"

"Son," she said, "that is the devil trying to discourage you and make you give up. You remember one thing as long as you live: Think about how you felt when the man of God prayed for you in the Name of Jesus. You received your healing then. But you have been sick for months. You lost your strength while lying in bed. It will take you some time to get it back."

Time proved that she was right. It took a little while, but I eventually felt my strength returning and within two months of my healing I delivered my first sermon. It was more like a testimony, but it had God's Word in it, too. Two souls were saved hearing that short message.

Later, my parents took me to the Sugg Clinic in Ada, Oklahoma. There my lungs were fluoroscoped sound as a dollar. The doctors told me, "You just forget you ever had tuberculosis." Later, samples of my blood and spittle were sent to the Oklahoma State Hospital. The report: No tuberculosis found!

From poverty to a runaway . . . from deathbed to healing . . . it all combined to make me a preacher. My first sermon was short, but it was a start. I often think about what would have happened, if, while leaning up against the house, I had accepted the doubt, given up my healing, reclaimed the tuberculosis, and gone back to bed. I believe I would never have risen from that bed again.

The millions of souls who have been saved, the hundreds of thousands of sick people who have been made well, all the many seeds of faith we have been able to plant, the hundreds of thousands of phone calls to the Prayer Tower and the millions of letters to this ministry over the years, the students and graduates of Oral Roberts University taking God's healing power into every man's world, the outreach through our television ministry . . . what would have happened to all these had I given up and gone back to my deathbed?

In our crusades in the big tent and auditoriums, we often sang the words of Stuart Hamblen's great song, "It is no secret what God can do. What He's done for others, He'll do for you. . . ." And we still sing it. Have faith in God. The same Jesus Who delivered me from the bed of affliction and death will deliver you, too, as you make Him the Source of your physical supply.

I do not feel I was anyone special, but I learned God is a good God and no problem is too big for Him to solve.

DON'T GIVE UP — REACH UP! I believe as you hook up to God, your Source, the answer is at your fingertips.

NO MATTER WHAT KIND OF PROBLEM YOU FACE . . . FROM A BROKEN HOME TO A BROKEN HEART . . . FROM BROKEN HEALTH TO A BROKEN FINANCIAL CONDITION . . . TO BROKEN FAITH . . . REMEMBER, THE GOD WHO TOOK A TEENAGE BOY WITHOUT HOPE, DYING FROM TUBERCULOSIS AND THEN PERFORMED A MIRACLE IN HIS LIFE . . . WHO

CONTINUES PERFORMING MIRACLES IN HIS LIFE, WILL PERFORM MIRACLES FOR YOU, TOO! AND, MOST IMPORTANT, DON'T GIVE UP ON GOD AS YOUR SOURCE — THE SOURCE OF YOUR PHYSICAL SUPPLY!

Make Him your **PHYSICAL SOURCE.**
Make Him your **FINANCIAL SOURCE.**
And, above ALL,
Make Him your **SPIRITUAL SOURCE.**

THE SOURCE OF YOUR TOTAL SUPPLY.

CHAPTER 4

THE SCRIPTURE THAT SHOOK MY SOUL

"Beloved, I wish above all things that thou mayest prosper and be in health, even as thy soul prospers" — III John 2.

I've read *III John 2* more times than I can count. In fact, I've literally based my healing ministry on that Scripture, and I've tried to build a foundation for my life on that Scripture. Recently, God drew me back to where it all began for me in *III John 2*. God asked me, "Oral Roberts, am I your Source?" That gripped my soul. I mean, I've preached on God as my Source for about 44 years, but God shook me back to my roots in Him and asked me all over again. I reflected back to when it all began inside Oral Roberts . . .

As a young man in college, pastoring a small church and with a young family to support, I struggled to make ends meet. I never had enough time for all that I needed to do and I certainly never had enough money. I mean we would go through the grocery store and pick out what we needed, and by the time we added up what our needs were and added up what our money was, Evelyn and I would end up putting one item after another back on the shelf because we did not have enough money to buy it all. Now, I'm not talking about frills or extras, I'm talking about the basics — food money. I loved God with all my heart, soul, and strength, and I believed He was a healing God since I had experienced the miracle of healing from tuberculosis in my own body at age 17. But I never seemed to grasp that God, through His Son Jesus Christ, could supply **all** of my needs. I mean, I never considered God <u>as my Source</u> for all my needs to be met in every area of my life. In the church I grew up in, God was not regarded as our Source. We were taught to be poor and humble in order to serve God. In order to serve God as a **meek** man, I believed I had to be a **weak** man. But I was so poor and humble that Evelyn and I nearly starved.

Then one day, on my way to catch the bus to the university, I realized that I had failed to do what I always did every morning before class. I forgot to start the day out by reading the Scripture. I ran back into the house, opened my Bible, and I quickly saw it fell open to *III John 2.*

I had read the Bible through many times, including the New Testament alone more than 100 times. I had read *III John 2* before, but it never registered in my soul like it did that day. Suddenly, these were no longer just words on a page, but life for my spirit as I shouted, *"Beloved I wish above all things that thou mayest prosper and be in health, even as thy soul prospers."* These words became health to my flesh and strength to my bones. They became reality to Oral Roberts. I ran to find Evelyn and immediately told her what I had just read. She said, "Oral, is that in the Bible?" I replied, "Evelyn, read it for yourself." So she took my Bible and read, *"Beloved, I wish above all things that thou mayest prosper and be in health, even as thy soul prospers."*

For the first time the revelation of that verse hit me. God wanted me to prosper — TO PROSPER — not just to have enough to scrape by, but TO PROSPER. This was a totally new thought to me. Then it says, *"and be in health"* — not just get healed, but to live an abundant life filled with good health, and all of this was according to as our souls prospered. Little did we realize that history was being made that day. From that moment, all of my study of the Word of God came to a climax. From that time, I understood that the principle of *III John 2* runs all through the Bible and everything I have done in my ministry has been based on this Scripture of God's highest wish for His people. God is truly the Source of my supply. This is not only true for me, but it is true for you as well!

The purpose for this book is to teach. It is to explain to you a system that God set up to work for you on your behalf — and to work properly when we get the formula right. God wants us to be **WHOLE,** to be complete. That's why *III John 2* talks of the three areas of our lives, financial, physical, and spiritual — *"Beloved, I wish above all things that thou mayest prosper and be in health, even as thy soul prospereth."*

All the things you will experience in life will fall somewhere into these three categories. If you don't get a stable, solid rock foundation for all these areas of your life, then no matter how hard you try to succeed, I believe you will crumble somewhere. No matter how high up you seem to go, unless there is a stable foundation to build on, eventually things will come crumbling down.

When a manufacturer makes a product, it's because he has a purpose in mind to begin with. When the product is finished, the manufacturer, or the MAKER, has learned what will work and what will not work concerning his product.

When God made us, He knew what would work and what would not work for our lives. He created the product from scratch. He put in all the right ingredients to cause His product to work the way He, the manufacturer, structured it to work in the first place. *The only way it won't work is if we mess up the system.* God created us to work properly, to prosper and be in health even as our soul prospers according to *III John 2.* Yet, if we don't get the parts right, the system won't function properly as OUR manufacturer, <u>OUR</u> <u>MAKER</u> intended.

<u>I</u> <u>WROTE</u> <u>THIS</u> <u>BOOK</u> <u>WITH</u> <u>YOU</u> <u>IN</u> <u>MIND.</u> God said that He wants your life to be exceedingly, abundantly above anything you could ask or think, but you've got to do it His way by making Him **THE SOURCE OF YOUR TOTAL SUPPLY.**

Perhaps one of the greatest revelations concerning the magnitude of *III John 2* happened to me while sitting in a hamburger restaurant here in Tulsa. Richard, Lindsay and I had just ordered lunch, and while we were waiting for our food, Lindsay began to discuss this Scripture and asked my point of view concerning the portion that says *"As thy soul prospers."* As I began to explain my understanding of this, Lindsay drew a Christmas tree and was making reference to getting to the top of the tree where the star was, where the light was, in essence, reaching up to Jesus — the Light of the world. As she was building up to the top, the thought hit me about the meaning, the full magnitude of this Scripture as I believe God would have us understand it spiritually, physically and financially.

The best way I can illustrate this is to explain just how God showed this to me. As I was looking at this picture of the Christmas tree, I saw inside the tree not the lights and decorations, but the building blocks of a strong spiritual foundation for our lives. A foundation is laid beginning with the three areas of our life, spiritual, physical, and financial. Then, as we connect the financial man with the spiritual man, we build a strong foundation in our life allowing us to go up higher in God.

The same is true as we connect our physical man with our spiritual man making God the Source of our health and physical well-being. Again, our foundation becomes stronger, and we move higher. As we stabilize our financial man and physical man by connecting those areas to the Spirit of God, we are building our lives on a solid, unshakable foundation so we can move into the health and prosperity of *III John 2* that God intended for each one of us.

Friend, for so many years I've seen people, even in the Body of Christ, with their lives disconnected from the true Source, lacking a solid rock foundation. They might allow God to rule in their physical man, but not in their finances, or they might allow God to be Lord of their finances, but leave Him out as Lord of their soul, or they never let Him be Lord of either their physical or financial man. But friend, I believe Jesus wants to be **LORD OF ALL!** I believe with all my heart that *III John 2* can become reality in our lives, and God's greatest wish for our lives — your life and mine — can come true!

One of the best real-life examples of this Scripture I've ever heard was told to me recently by my daughter-in-law, Lindsay, and it was concerning her daughter — my 6-year-old granddaughter, Jordan. As Lindsay was busy going about her daily work one day, Jordan came into the room where she was cleaning a closet and desperately needed her mother's attention. Lindsay said she saw such frustration in Jordan that she stopped and sat down right there and said, "Jordan, what's wrong?" Jordan explained how she was trying to learn spelling words and vowel sounds from a book Lindsay had given her. She came across the word "B-e-a-r" and couldn't understand how two vowels, "e" and "a," made one sound.

She really was puzzled, but then out of the blue, she jumped up and exclaimed, "I can get this 'B' word because I learned my 'I' letter!" Confused by this, Lindsay asked, "What do you mean?" Because Jordan had been taught the alphabet in Scriptures, she instantly replied, "I can learn the 'B' word because of the 'I' letter. **'I CAN DO ALL THINGS THROUGH CHRIST WHO STRENGTHENS ME.'** That means with Christ I can learn my vowels."

While Lindsay was rejoicing with Jordan in her discovery, God impressed Lindsay with the fact that this was *III John 2* in actuality. Lindsay said that God showed her that as Jordan's soul, her spirit man, would prosper in Jesus Christ, then every other area of her life would follow along and prosper and be in health. If her soul or spirit man was weak or down or not prospering, then neither would the other areas of her life. But as she prospers in the Lord and builds herself up in God, then she has a solid rock foundation to build on in every other area of her life.

As I heard this story, it hit me about you, my friends and Partners. I want so much for you to get a revelation of the goodness of God according to *III John 2* and just what He has in store for your life, in every area — spiritually, physically, financially. *Third John 2* covers it all. *"Beloved, I wish above all things that you prosper* [financially and in your family] *and be in health* [physically], *even as thy soul prospers* [spiritually]."* God said He wished above all things that we prosper spiritually, physically, and financially. Friend, if that's <u>His</u> highest wish, then why aren't <u>we</u> doing it? Well, I believe it's as *John 10:10* says, the thief — or the devil — comes for no other purpose but to steal, kill, and destroy, but Jesus came to settle it once and for all. He finished *John 10:10* by saying, *"I am come that you might have life and have it more abundantly."*

Friend, it's time we take God at His Word. If Jesus came to give us life *(John 10:10)*, to destroy the works of the devil *(I John 3:8)* that we may prosper and be in health *(III John 2);* let's make a decision to do it. Jesus has already come. He's done His part. He was sent to us as a baby in a manger, He had a ministry of miracles, then was crucified, died, and buried, and on the third day He was resurrected so we could live out the promises of God.

I thank God that He sent His Son in the form of a baby in a manger and that we celebrate His miracle birth at Christmas. But, let's never forget **WHY HE CAME.** He didn't come so we could enjoy neon lights in a shopping mall and tinsel in a tree. That's how the world has reduced His miracle birth. But, December 25 doesn't represent a winter holiday, it represents **DELIVERANCE!** Deliverance from the world's system to God's saving, healing, abundant, heavenly system. God sent His Son, not merely to

41

be born, but to die for the redemption of sins — your sins and mine. And He didn't stop there. He came to destroy sickness and disease and the oppression of the devil. His resurrection means our **DELIVERANCE** — spiritually, physically, and financially — in every area of life.

I'm burning with a fire in my soul today to get a message to you, my friends and Partners, that our deliverance is through the miraculous birth, life, death, and resurrection of Jesus Christ. As we build our foundation in Him, all other areas of our life will prosper even *"as our souls prosper."* As we continue to learn how this is for each of us, I keep reminding you to:

Make Him your **PHYSICAL SOURCE.**
Make Him your **FINANCIAL SOURCE.**
    And, above ALL,
Make Him your **SPIRITUAL SOURCE.**

THE SOURCE OF YOUR TOTAL SUPPLY.

CHAPTER 5

THE CHILDREN WHO SHOOK MY SOUL

Read these power-packed MIRACLE TESTIMONIES and let your faith arise to believe for God to be your Source of PHYSICAL SUPPLY!

Jacob Garrison

"I felt like my whole world was crumbling around me. That was my baby. They told me he had no chance of surviving."

Spinal meningitis is a very dangerous and contagious childhood disease. When Jacob Garrison contracted this disease, it was a devastating blow to his entire family.

JACOB'S GRANDFATHER: There were all kinds of thoughts going through our minds when we heard Jacob's diagnosis. Of course, the first thing that comes to your mind, you look up, "Lord God, this child is very precious to us. Don't take him away from us."

JACOB'S MOTHER: The doctors told me Jacob had no chance of surviving. And I said, "Yes, he does." I got on the phone and called my mom. I was so in a panic I couldn't remember the phone number to Richard Roberts. So I said, "Mom, please call Richard Roberts in Tulsa."

JACOB'S GRANDMOTHER: I called Tulsa [the Prayer Tower], and asked for prayer. I wasn't upset. I wasn't nervous. I hung up and then I went about getting ready to go to the hospital. And then my daughter called and said, "Mom, you'd better hurry. They don't expect Jacob to live. He's on life support." I said, "Honey, he's going to be OK. I already called the Prayer Tower in Tulsa."

MOTHER: The doctors told us that he would be hooked up to these machines for two weeks. He had life support. He had IVs in both arms. They had him strapped to a bed and he was on a respirator. They said that it would be a long time before they could get him off. He didn't have any vital signs. All this was happening to him, but still, 30 hours later, he was miraculously restored to health. They took him off the life support, and he was singing and just happy and bubbly like his old self. The doctors couldn't believe it. I said, "That's the power of God." And they said, "Well, I guess you're right, because there's only so much that medicine can do."

GRANDMOTHER: He's a normal, healthy, little kid; he's all boy. And, I mean, it's amazing. We look at him and get a lump in the throat because we almost lost him. But I think God has other plans for him.

Beau Van Geffen

What started out as a quiet family vacation in the Rocky Mountains in Colorado turned into a nightmare. Miles from the nearest phone or hospital, Tom and Becky Van Geffen's youngest son Beau was bitten by a poisonous snake and was near death.

TOM: It's like the doctor said it just yesterday; it's branded in my brain. "Mr. Van Geffen, in all probability," he said, "your son's going to die this evening. You're going to have to deal with that."

My first impression when I heard my son screaming was that he had seen a snake and it was probably close enough to him to scare him. So I just jogged down through the rocks, and when I got to him, I picked him up and he started throwing up. He looked straight up and to the left, then he went limp in my arms. I thought he'd died.

Beau was taken by ambulance to Estes Park, where they immediately began pumping antivenin into him. Because of the seriousness of his condition, Beau had to be flown to Children's Hospital in Denver, some 75 miles away.

BECKY: By the time they got him to Children's Hospital, Beau was unconscious and the doctors put him on life support. He was in very, very critical condition. Within the next 48 hours, we would know if he would survive or not. They ended up giving Beau 33 vials of antivenin. The most they had ever given to any person, adult or child, was about 15 vials.

TOM: The doctors had this antivenin machine stuck in his foot, and the syringe was huge. Antivenin is horse serum. It's a poison in itself, but it's the only thing known that will neutralize the venom of a snake. So they immediately began treating him for the serum sickness. The offsprings of the antivenin are mental retardation and all kinds of horrible side effects and neurological damage.

Beau's chances for ever again living a normal life were slim. However, Becky knew that God was their Source. She knew what they needed to do.

BECKY: We both agreed that we needed prayer, that we needed an army of prayer to get Beau through this. Naturally, this was in the middle of the night, and the first place I thought of calling was the Abundant Life Prayer Group on the Oral Roberts University campus.

TOM: A lady answered the phone and I told her who I was. "I'm at Children's Hospital in Denver. My son's going to die of a rattlesnake bite." She immediately took over. You know, she took control of the conversation. She started praying, and I just listened and cried and kept crying. And then when I hung up the phone I had a strange feeling, it was so peaceful, you could cut it with a knife. That's why I know now the power of prayer works.

BECKY: That day things began to turn around and Beau's swelling started going down. He became conscious, and from that point on his body just began to heal. Everything they had said was going to happen, did not happen. Even the doctor came up to me and said, "You do know that you're looking at a miracle, don't you?" I said, "Yes, I do." And we brought Beau home again. Within three days he was out in the front yard playing soccer — miraculously healed. He's never had one problem since. The fear has never manifested in any way, and he's not had any nightmares. He's just been totally healthy, and we just praise the Lord. God was truly faithful in every way to us throughout the whole experience.

Joshua Wilson

Jim and Julie Wilson of Broken Arrow, Oklahoma, had everything going for them—a successful career and a beautiful home. Then tragedy struck their only son, Joshua, and it seemed their world was caving in.

JULIE: Our doctor got this horrible look on his face when he was examining Joshua — it was the kind of look a mother doesn't like to see. We found out later after a series of tests, Joshua had neuroblastoma, a form of cancer.

JIM: When the doctors told us that Josh had cancer, my first reaction was a spirit of fear that came over me. As we got into the treatments and so forth, the fear stayed with me for some time and I kept trying to get rid of it.

JULIE: As the days went on and Joshua took the chemotherapy, he got sick a lot. We couldn't take him out of the house, because he was so susceptible to illness. He had two rounds of chemother-

apy when he was sick with pneumonia. This was
definitely the trial of our lives.

Jim and Julie were not alone. Through the sup-
portive prayers of friends and the Abundant Life
Prayer Group, they began to see God's healing power
at work in their own lives.

JULIE: I think being a former student at Oral
Roberts University and with all the teaching that I
learned while I was there, I knew where I needed to
go when crisis struck. I needed to go to God. I didn't
depend on myself or my friends or my family. At
that point I remembered, and I picked up the phone
while I was in the hospital, called the Abundant
Life Prayer Group and I asked them for prayer.
And the dearest, sweetest person answered that
phone. She took my need on just like it was her
own. She understood. She wept on the phone with
me. And we gave Joshua to the Lord. After I called
the Abundant Life Prayer Group, they brought our
needs before Richard and Lindsay while they were
on the television program. And they prayed for
Josh.

LINDSAY: I talked to Julie at about 10:30 one
night. She said they had discovered this cancerous
tumor on Joshua, and that she was at the hospital
and they were going to do surgery on her little
nine-week-old baby. I remember praying on the program the next morning. At the time, my baby was
exactly the same age. I just got mad at the devil
and said, "Joshua, we're still expecting a miracle
for you today. Right now, in the Name of Jesus, I
come against any sickness or disease that holds
your body down. In Jesus' Name, devil, I'm talking
to you . . . ."

The Wilsons did touch Heaven, and through
their faith in God, their precious son, Joshua, was

miraculously and completely healed of cancer.

JULIE: If we hadn't had all of these people supporting us through prayer, things would have looked pretty bleak, and we might have just given up.

Today, Joshua is able to run and play, and now has a little brother, Jonathan — perfectly whole and perfectly normal.

JOSHUA: Jesus healed me and He can heal you, too.

Make Him your **PHYSICAL SOURCE.**
Make Him your **FINANCIAL SOURCE.**
    And, above ALL,
Make Him your **SPIRITUAL SOURCE.**

THE SOURCE OF YOUR TOTAL SUPPLY.

II. GOD IS THE SOURCE OF YOUR FINANCIAL SUPPLY

6. DAVE AND BARBARA: "YOU DON'T TALK TO GOD LIKE THAT . . . I THOUGHT THE PRAYER TOWER WAS GOING TO FALL DOWN!"

7. "BUT MY GOD SHALL SUPPLY *ALL YOUR NEEDS*"

8. KAREN: "I HAD $15 LEFT AND GAVE $10 OF IT TO GOD."

CHAPTER 6

DAVE AND BARBARA: "YOU DON'T TALK TO GOD LIKE THAT . . . I THOUGHT THE PRAYER TOWER WAS GOING TO FALL DOWN!"

BARBARA: I got drunk one night and I went to an old-time, apostolic, Pentecostal revival. I had my hair sort of shaved off and went right up the front aisle. I walked in that church, I got saved, and the Holy Ghost set me on fire. It almost split up the whole family. I was just instantaneously so hungry for God that it didn't seem normal, but it is normal with God. To this day, I don't think I've seen anything like it.

At church I read a big sign that said, "You're the only feet, the only hands, and the only mouth that Jesus has down here," and it got my heart. My husband said, "You can go get drunk, you can go have an affair, but you're not [I remember he hit the table] going to go to another church. If you do, then find your clothes outside." I said "God, what's happening?" I had thought everything was going to be all right.

I got this book, *How to Get Through Your*

Struggles, from Oral Roberts, and I started reading it step by step by step, really like a child. I said, "Well, I don't have any money, but we got an invitation to go to a seminar, and, God, this is what I'm going to do. I'll teach Sunday school; that's my seed. And I'll expect." I think we needed $1,200 for tickets and everything. They were going to provide room and board, and so I said, "David, this is what I'm going to do." He said, "Yeah, we'll go, but you'll never get that money. That junk doesn't work." I said, "God, You heard him. I don't know how You're going to do it, but You said that I was going to reap what I sowed."

Every day I'd wait and wait and wait, and finally I went and got the tickets. I reserved them until the last day, and then I had to bring in the money. I said, "God, the money's not here yet." But all of a sudden, we got the money, and we found ourselves on the plane the next day. Dave was furious and angry, but I was so excited.

When we got to ORU, we walked into the Mabee Center where they had registration. They had thousands of people and someone came up to me and said, "What has Oral Roberts' ministry done for your life?" I told them the story and they said, "We're going to get back with you later. We'd like to televise you."

My husband had a fit. I said, "God, I didn't ask this lady to come up to me." But Dave was going to leave. He said, "I'm getting on the plane. I'm getting out of here. I'm not staying. You stay down here. I'm not taking this anymore." I said, "God, what's happening? He wasn't like this."

Oral Roberts spoke that night on how God can help you with your business. Well, Dave's a businessman, a contractor, and we weren't selling any houses, so this message got his ear. Then there was a pledge service for a building project in the ministry, and I think we pledged $1,200 for the year. That was a huge mountain for us. We were scared and shaking when we put in that pledge.

That night after Oral spoke about how Jesus can help in your business, we went to the Prayer Tower, and my husband began to fight with himself. You could see an actual fight. He was saying, "You can't have my business. That's mine." He was talking to God! Boy, <u>I thought the Prayer Tower was going to fall down. You don't talk to God like that!</u> Before he knew it, Dave was weeping hysterically. "Take the business. Take my life. I'll do anything. I surrender my life." My husband was a changed man, absolutely changed.

The next day we went for the interview that the ministry wanted. They were going to interview me. Dave purposely didn't even shave, but they put the lights on him and me, and then shut the lights off on me. They just interviewed him. He was absolutely changed, and he's never been the same. We sold seven houses that year which was exceedingly, abundantly beyond anything we could think or comprehend.

DAVE: I know the Holy Spirit came in and just totally, totally changed me. I challenged God. That's a hard thing to do, but I believed and I didn't believe. I'd see and I didn't see. But that night when Oral Roberts spoke about what God can do in your business, bells went off in my head. That's what I had to hear. It was a struggle, I can't even explain it. I knew that I was wrong, I knew that I was fighting. But you can only put up so much and then God just takes over. I said, "God, You can have the house. You can have my kids. You can have my wife. You can have me. You can have anything. I just want peace. I just want to see more of You." And that was it.

I cried and I cried and I cried like you cannot believe. It was a SUPERNATUIRAL, SPIRITUAL SURGERY that was going on inside me from the top of my head to the bottom of my feet. It doesn't matter if I understand it or can explain it. It was something that changed me and supernaturally set me on fire inside, even though I may not show it on the outside. I made God the boss of my business. I only work for Him. He tells me what to do and I go do it.

Thank God, the first thing I learned from Oral was how to give and receive. How to be in seedtime and harvest time, how to plant something and expect God to give it back. When I heard that 13 years ago, I said, "Huh, that doesn't make sense," but lots of biblical things don't make sense. That's okay. If God says it, I believe it and that's all I care about. I praise God because Oral is so obedient. If he weren't, we wouldn't be here today. This ministry really changed our lives.

It's something that God instilled into my heart. It's like God told me, "David, go help My son, Oral Roberts, My servant. Help him, pray for him, lift him financially. Whatever it is, back him up." It doesn't have to be just through finances. Lots of it is through prayer.

I'm just a steward, or a servant, helping another servant. No one can take that away from me. I started my business in 1980 with $5. I've got the checkbook that shows you the $5. People thought we were crazy.

It doesn't matter. We're not ashamed of the Gospel of Jesus Christ and we're not ashamed to tell others that God is our Source. He is a good God!

Make Him your **PHYSICAL SOURCE.**
Make Him your **FINANCIAL SOURCE.**
    And, above ALL,
Make Him your **SPIRITUAL SOURCE.**

THE SOURCE OF YOUR TOTAL SUPPLY.

CHAPTER 7

"BUT MY GOD SHALL SUPPLY *ALL* YOUR NEEDS"

There was an antique dealer who was always traveling around, going into little towns to look for bargains. He came to this one small town and walked up and down the street, till he came to a store that sold a little of everything. He looked in the windows but couldn't see anything, then he looked in the doorway and saw a cat drinking milk out of an old bowl. He stood there watching because he liked cats.

As he watched, he noticed that that wasn't just an old bowl. He said, "Why, that's an antique. That thing is worth a lot of money. And this old boy that runs the store, probably doesn't know that." So he walked over and picked up the cat and stroked it. And he said, "You know, I've always loved cats. I've been looking for a cat just like this. Would you sell me this cat?" And the man said, "Sure, I'll sell you anything in this store if you've got the money." And the antique dealer said, "Well, how much?" The merchant said, "If you give me $25, the cat's yours."

So he paid him, picked up the cat, and started out, then he turned and came back and picked up the bowl and said, "Oh, by the way, I noticed this cat was drinking out of this old bowl. It's probably not worth much. He's used to it. I'll just take this old bowl with the cat." And the merchant said, "You put that bowl down. That's the best cat-seller I've ever had."

Now those two fellows represent a lot of Christians and a lot of people who each are trying to get to the other one first. These people haven't heard the message of Seed-Faith yet. God never intended for any one of us to get ahead in life by tearing someone else down, by beating someone out of a fair deal, by using someone else's head as a stepping-stone to the top. God wants us to prosper, to be the head and not the tail, to be above and not below *(Deuteronomy 28:13)*. But He never intended for us to get there by the world's system. He gave us a way to prosper, but only according to His system in His <u>Word.</u>

Luke 6:38 tells us that as we give, it shall be given to us again. *Galatians 6:7,9* tells us, *"Be not deceived; God is not mocked: For whatsoever a man soweth, that shall he also reap. And let us not be weary in well doing: for in due season we shall reap, if we faint not."* God told us that He gave us the power to get wealth *(Deuteronomy 8:18)* and that He would bless us and <u>make</u> us a <u>blessing</u> *(Hebrews 6:14)*. These are God's thoughts regarding our success. The world has its system of "prosperity," but it differs greatly from God's system of "<u>biblical</u> prosperity."

What I want to share with you concerning biblical prosperity is written in Paul's letter to the church at Philippi regarding giving and receiving, sowing and reaping, seedtime and harvest through which God will bless you, and in blessing you, He will MAKE you a blessing. God gave us sowing and reaping throughout His Word from Genesis through

Revelation. He said in *Genesis 8:22* as long as the earth remains there will be seedtime and harvest.

We know that the Apostle Paul taught this wherever he traveled to establish churches and teach them how to go on with God and get all their needs met. But <u>no church</u>, no group of believers COMMUNICATED or <u>felt what he felt</u> concerning giving and receiving as the Philippian church did *(Philippians 4:15)*. But, because of the Philippians' seed of faith or <u>faithful</u> sowing into God's work, Paul was able to teach them the great scriptural lesson in living their lives based on sowing their seed to God. And, he could also teach them how to **receive from God** so that God could indeed supply all their need according to His riches in glory by Christ Jesus *(Philippians 4:19)*. By teaching them both giving AND receiving, he was teaching them how to make God the <u>SOURCE</u> of their total supply.

Biblical Principles for Biblical Prosperity

This chapter is about trusting God as your Source for all your financial needs. We're going to open up what God has revealed in His Word, and the revelation knowledge He's revealed to me concerning these passages. In the 44 years of this healing ministry, I have tried to live within the framework of the Scripture, all of the Bible, but in a particular sense the Scriptures on Seed-Faith. There has been much difficulty as people have tried to understand the miracle of Seed-Faith. They've grasped all of it, half of it, a little of it, grabbed at it, held onto it, had it for a while, lost it, and all kinds of things.

There have been times I admit I have shown a weakness and I didn't bear down at certain points like I should have or I didn't offer it often enough. I thought if I taught the principle of Seed-Faith a few times people would understand and practice their faith and they would actually get ahold of it as a lifestyle as I, and so many others, have done. But sometimes, under the oppressing powers of satan, I would back away. Now after 44 years, I am honored to let it all out. I'm going to explain to you what I wholly believe, what I've tried to practice. And when I practiced it, it worked in my spirit, mind, body, family, and my entire ministry.

I know that I know that I know that this is one of the reasons I was called by God. I believe that if I communicate God's <u>biblical</u> principles regarding <u>biblical</u> prosperity, and you really put God's <u>biblical</u> principles of <u>biblical</u> prosperity into practice every day of your life, that you will be a changed person and you will have the finances to meet your needs. Besides that, I believe God will be touching your body with miraculous healings, and touching your family.

Read *Philippians 4:13-19*, and mark around those verses with your pen or pencil. Underscore the words that are emphasized. I want this to be one of the major instruments through which you see God as your Source, meeting all your financial needs — because if you get all your financial needs met, I believe that could help solve some of your physical needs that come from lack of money. If the worry, anxiety, fear and stress over money are eating up your physical body on the inside, or gnawing at your stomach, or trying to drive you out of your mind, then <u>STOP</u> right now. Ask God to give you <u>His</u> divine revelation concerning *Philippians 4:13-19* that applies directly to your life, your family, your circumstances, <u>YOUR TOTAL BEING</u>.

Carefully and prayerfully read these words from the Apostle Paul. These are not Oral Roberts' words, but Paul's divinely inspired words to believers and to the Church. Try to picture this great apostle of God as he writes, *"I can <u>do all things</u> through Christ which strengtheneth me. <u>Notwithstanding</u> ye have well done, that ye did <u>communicate</u> with my affliction."* The word affliction here means **need**. The Philippians communicated with Paul regarding his needs. *"Now ye Philippians* [you believers in the city called Philippi] *know also, that in the beginning of the gospel, when I departed from Macedonia* [the northern part of the nation of Greece], *no church communicated with me as concerning <u>giving</u> and <u>receiving</u>, but ye only. For even in Thessalonica ye sent once and again* [meaning again and again and again] *unto my necessity. Not because I desire a gift: but I desire fruit that may abound to your account. But I have all, and abound: I am full, having received of Epaphroditus the things which were sent from you, an odour of a sweet smell, a sacrifice acceptable, well-pleasing to God. But my God shall supply all your need according to his riches in glory by Christ Jesus."* Notice, in particular, verse 13, *"I can do all things through Christ which strengtheneth me."*

The Foundation for Biblical Prosperity

I cannot begin to number the amount of people who have quoted that verse out of context. Preachers and lay people everywhere have taken this one verse, left out all the qualifying Scriptures around it that cause it to really come to pass, and have built much of their faith on this one verse taken out of context. In a pinch, without any structure laid or foundation built, they fall back on this

Scripture as if to use it for a quick way out: *"I can do all things through Christ who strengthens me."* They can quote it, they can recite it, BUT THEY DON'T READ THE REST OF IT. They skip verses 14-18 and hurry to get to verse 19, which is the verse that nearly every Christian quotes: *"But my God shall supply all your need according to his riches in glory by Christ Jesus."*

I've said it countless numbers of times. Maybe you've also said it scores or hundreds of times, and it's been said to you, too. But I believe with all of my heart that it will not work out of context. It won't, or all of us would already have all of our needs met. Verses 13 and 19 quoted out of context are like two pieces of bread with no meat in the middle — and you don't buy sandwiches like that.

Now let's look carefully at this so we can make verse 13 come to pass, so verse 19 will also come to pass, because I want more than anything in my life to be able to do all the things through Christ Who strengthens me. And I want all my needs met . . . not half of them . . . I want them all met, in my soul, in my body, in my finances, in my family, in the work that I'm to do. I want them all met. I don't want satan to look me in the eye and say, "You can't have this need met." I want my God to supply my needs and all your needs. In the Name of Jesus Christ of Nazareth, I want you to see a breakthrough, a deliverance, a total victory in every area of your life — spiritually, physically and financially — as you make God the SOURCE OF YOUR TOTAL SUPPLY.

Miracle Potential

Look at verse 13. *"I can do all things through Christ who strengtheneth me."* What is Paul talking

64

about? There were times when Paul did not do all things. As you study his life and read his writings, he will tell you what he's striving for, what he's reaching for, what he wants done . . . which hadn't been done. But he knew that if he reached a certain place, if he could get people to cooperate with him, then this verse — which is filled with miracle potential — could happen.

"I can [definition of ability; possession of a specified power, right or means; possession of a specified capacity or skill] *do all things through Christ who strengtheneth me."* That's Paul's potential talking. I can rise to the height that God ordained for me. I can do everything that God planned for me with His strengthening power.

Now notice verse 14. *"Notwithstanding,"* which means however, or in addition to that. He's saying, "I can't do it by myself," and nobody can. We need one another. In *I Corinthians 12:21*, Paul writes that the different members of a body cannot say they do not need one another. We have to have one another to function as the Body of Christ on this earth. You can't even produce a baby by yourself. It takes two. And often it takes a support group behind the two. *"I can do all things through Christ who strengtheneth me."* That's my potential. That's your potential.

But that's not the end of the story. If I stop there, out of context of what the ENTIRE passage is teaching, it won't work, because it's not complete. It's like only half of the equation. *"Notwithstanding* [however] *ye have well done* [or you've done well], *that ye did communicate with my affliction,"* or my need.

65

You Do Well to Communicate

Now notice the word "communicate" and underline it. Communication is what I'm trying to do
right now. But communication doesn't stop with
me. Communication is in the one I'm speaking
with. If you don't understand what I'm saying, if I
don't get through to you, you've not been communicated with. You heard the words. It's like saying to
your little boy or your little girl, "You do this, you
do that," and they don't do a thing. They don't carry
out your orders. Then you didn't communicate with
them. But once they got the message and they
understood the blessings and the other conse-
quences, they're more likely to feel communicated
with. They come back and say, "I understand," or
"Yes, I did it." *"Notwithstanding ye have well done,
that ye did communicate with my affliction."* Paul is
saying, "My potential is that I can do all things
with Christ strengthening me, however, you have
done well, because you communicated with me.
Even though I've got the potential of doing all
things, your communication with me makes the dif-
ference."

Philippi was a Roman colony, the chief city of
the northern part of the nation of Greece on the
Mediterranean Sea, and that northern part is
called now, like it was then, Macedonia. And in
Macedonia, Philippi was the chief city. *"Now ye
Philippians* [believers in Philippi] *know* [underline
the word "know"] *also* [beyond just communication,
it means there is something else that you know]. *Ye
Philippians know also, that in the beginning of the
gospel, when I departed from Macedonia,"* or, in
other words, when I left after I first brought the
Gospel to Macedonia, *"no church,"* and he meant
none of the churches that he had established, *"no*

church communicated with me." No church got through to me. They may have said words like, "I'll do it," but they never got through to him. You probably know what it means for someone to get through to you. You've heard them say words, and you knew in your heart that doesn't mean a thing. But you knew when it meant something, the communication got through and you could act. Paul said, *"No church communicated with me as concerning giving."* Most people stop right there. And people are so worn out in being beat over the head to give, but nobody would feel like that if they would read the whole thing and get what it really is that God is <u>communicating.</u> *"No church communicated with me as concerning giving and receiving."* Giving <u>and</u> receiving. Giving <u>AND</u> receiving. *"But ye only."* You may think, Oh, could that have happened to the great Apostle Paul? I thought everything was just wonderful back then. It was not all just wonderful. It was just wonderful in parts.

Paul's Need in Persecution

"But ye only. For when in Thessalonica [a city not far from Philippi] *ye sent once and again* [again and again and again] *unto my necessity."* Now, what's the story behind this? Read this portion carefully. When Paul and his associates, Silas and others, came into Philippi and preached the Gospel, they cast out a demon from a young woman, who through this demon could tell fortunes. A certain man had bought her and used her to tell the fortunes of people, and was getting rich as a result of her doing this. The girl was no longer a human being, no longer a free woman, but now she was possessed of this demon of the occult. The demons in her knew Paul and they made her run after Paul

and call on him because they knew that he was from God. Paul turned around and commanded that demon to come out of that girl in the Name of Jesus. And it came out of her. Suddenly, she was no longer under the occult, this present darkness. The demon spirits who knew so much could not reveal certain things to her about other people. As a result of this, the man who owned her lost his fortune, and he had Paul and Silas thrown into jail.

Now just think about Paul, and how great he was. That's the first thing we tend to think is how great he was, and how anointed he was. Imagine your local pastor has the exact same experience right in your hometown, and immediately they put him in jail. Do you see the point? Or perhaps, at the end of one of my messages at a chapel service on the campus of Oral Roberts University, some group of crooks misrepresents me to the local authorities, they rush in and grab me and throw me into jail alongside the local pastor. Then they beat us, and yet we were able to cling to God.

Well, they beat Paul and Silas, they jailed them, and yet, in the midnight hours, they sang. They sang and they prayed (getting into praise and worship), and God shook the earth, tore the prison walls apart and let them out, but not before they won the jailer to Jesus. They were able to put a church together; a body of believers. And then Paul said to his accusers, "I happen to be a Roman citizen, and I have the right to a trial. And you put me into jail without a hearing, without a trial." They knew what that meant, that Caesar could come down on that city. When they realized they'd made a mistake, they said, "Please, we're so sorry. Would you just please take your group and leave town? Please leave peaceably." And they left that little band of people they had won to Christ. And this young woman who had been delivered from demons was now among those believers.

They crossed the Aegean Sea over to a city called Thessalonica, which was named for Thessalonia, the sister of Alexander the Great (who conquered the world and founded the fourth world empire, and wept and died at the age of 33 because he had no more kingdoms to conquer). When Paul got to Thessalonica it was much like it was in Philippi. The persecution followed him. His afflictions or his needs became so severe that he had no place to stay and was beat upon nearly every day. In Thessalonica, Paul was apparently starved half to death. The enemies from Philippi continued to cross over and persecute him. This is why there was such depth and meaning in Paul's writing here when he said, "Now concerning giving and receiving, you Philippians know you are the only ones who sent to my necessity. You did it again and again, and you communicated with me *'concerning giving and receiving'.*"

Giving <u>and</u> Receiving

What he was saying was, "I taught you how to give and receive. I taught you that when you gave you were to receive, <u>that when you received you were to give, when you gave, you were to receive</u>. You would give and receive, and receive and give, and give and receive, and receive and give! When your left arm worked, your right arm worked. When your left foot moved, your right foot moved. And you gave and you received, and you received and you gave, and I taught you how to Seed-Faith your way through by staying in Philippi where they had tried to kill me.

"And you're the only ones in all the churches I established in Macedonia where I taught giving and receiving, that I was communicated with. I gave the communication before, but they weren't listening. They heard my words, but they never got a thing. But you communicated. You are the only ones who got the message on giving and receiving inside you. And you communicated back to me with <u>your</u> giving, because you knew you were going to <u>receive again</u> from God through the <u>seeds you sowed</u> to Him for the purpose of meeting my need so I could keep the Gospel going."

Well, Paul said, "You believers in Philippi are the only ones that I was able to communicate with." Notice what happened. Look at verse 16, *"For even in Thessalonica ye sent once and again unto my necessity."* They sent to a man of God that in most instances, wherever he turned, they would beat him or they'd throw him into jail or they'd run him out of town. And yet today, if one of us gets hit, other Christians get so offended and so intimidated that they begin to be just like the criticizers, or just like the secular media, just like the voice of the accuser instead of becoming the voice of the **Intercessor**. When Christians get hit, other Christians are to seek God and hear **HIS** voice and tune out the voice of the world.

Romans 8:7 says, *"The carnal mind is enmity against God."* The mind doesn't understand spiritual things, but the SPIRIT does! Jesus was persecuted and maligned and falsely accused, and He said if they treated Him that way, they'd treat us that way: "If you love me the world will hate you." (See *John 15:19.*) But then He also said in *Matthew 5:11,12, "Blessed are ye, when men shall revile you, and persecute you, and shall say all manner of evil against you falsely, for my sake. Rejoice, and be exceeding glad: for great is your reward in heaven: for so persecuted they the prophets which were before you."* Today many Christians want to find a church where there's comfort and safety. It's like masquerading around as a child of God. They wouldn't have lasted one second following Paul the Apostle. When they threw him into jail and beat him and bloodied him, how do you think a luke-warm Christian would respond? "I don't want to be mixed up in something like this."

I'll tell you now, the power of God is coming greater than it's ever come, and with it, some people are going to get mad and the devil will be enraged and we're going to see something again like what happened to Paul. But the glory will outweigh the suffering. And some people are going to get communicated with, and, through giving and receiving, be prepared for whatever happens. You can sum up all of Christianity, giving God your best, then receiving His best. And then you can do all things.

Ministry Motivation

Paul said in verses 16,17, *"For even in Thessalonica ye sent once and again unto my necessity. **Not because I desire a gift.**"* Now that's what he said. He put that in quickly because there's a certain place in the New Testament where he stated that they accused him of being in the Gospel, of preaching just for the money he would get out of it. And he said, "I want you to know I'm not saying this because I desire your gift. I have to have gifts. I have to have money, but that's not my motivating desire. That's not what my mind is on. That's not what I'm in it for."

71

Maybe a few really are in their work for God, even in the ministry, only for the money. I can't stop those who feel that way. Yet, you don't put every man or woman of God into a category of "all preachers." That's not true. It's like saying all doctors are in business for money, or all doctors are involved in malpractice, or all lawyers are crooked, or all this or all that. That's a total impossibility to put all people into the same category just because of the one thing they have in common: their profession.

Let me tell you, people can get offended and blame every man of God in the world when there's only a small group of ministers of the Gospel who may have gone bad. Otherwise, it wouldn't make the headlines, because the media only wants bad news. They don't write much about the good ones. But when something seemingly crooked comes by, that's on the front page or on a popular TV program, that's news. It seems they're not interested in the good, and certainly not the "Good News of the Gospel." Don't get carried away in fear because one or two people unfortunately fell into something. Maybe their hearts didn't even want it, but for some reason, they slipped and fell. If they're ministers, they still have the call. *Romans 11:29* says, *"For the gifts and calling of God are without repentance."* I mean, this is serious business. Pray for people who fall. Don't side with the accusers and those who want to destroy everything. They could turn against you, too! If that happened, you would want others to pray and believe God to help you.

Paul said, *"Not because I desire a gift."* As a man of God, I need money to carry out God's work. So does every other minister. So do you in whatever work you do. But I'm not in this Gospel because I desire money from anybody. That's not my motive.

"Not because I desire a gift." Paul was saying, "I don't desire this giving and receiving of yours just to get a gift for myself." And right there it sounds so good, doesn't it? We sound so humble and meek and everybody says, "That's the way you ought to be." *"But,"* he said. Let's get the rest of the meat in the sandwich. *"But I desire."* What is his desire? *"But I desire fruit that may abound to your account."* Where does fruit come from? From <u>seed</u>, doesn't it? Did you ever have any fruit that didn't come from a seed that was sown — what we call seedtime and harvest? Giving and receiving is the same as seedtime and harvest, sowing and reaping. You never ate a radish in your life for which the seed wasn't planted. You never ate an apple that didn't come from a seed that grew into an apple tree that produced fruit.

Your Overflowing Account

"I desire fruit that may abound to your account." Now get that word "abound." I married a school teacher, Evelyn Lutman. She's now Evelyn Roberts. Fifty-three years ago I "rescued" her from the classroom. She was making twice as much teaching as I was preaching, and she left it to marry me! I asked, "Evelyn, what does abound mean?" She said, "Overflowing." I picked up my dictionary and the first meaning of abounding that the dictionary had was overflowing. So I knew it was right because my former-school-teacher wife had told me first!

"And I desire fruit that may abound." Fruit that may overflow. This is what people in Christ have a hard time believing because the devil is trying to steal it from you and steal it from me. *"Fruit that may abound to your account."* What is an account? If you have a bank account, what is it? You put

money in there and you've got a bank account. And the more you put in, the larger the check you can write that doesn't bounce. *"Fruit that may abound to your account"* means that when you have a need, you can draw from your account with God. When I've been bolder in my approach to God, it's because I knew I had an account with God. But when I knew the account had dwindled down, and I sent up my check, it would bounce and God would say, "There's nothing in your account."

Now look at verse 18, and underline the word "abound." *"But I have all, and abound: I am full."* Now think of Paul. Imagine he's standing up here saying, "I have all. I abound. I'm full. I've got all the money I need, and it's overflowing." Would you stay and listen to him? Would you say he was in it for the money? Would you say he was sincere? Would you say he believed God and he walked with God and he got believers to get into giving and receiving, and suddenly he began to abound?

If I came in here with old worn-out clothes, after I had thumbed my way into town and I looked like yesterday's scarecrow, then I walk up in the pulpit, and I say, "Look at me. I'm a preacher. Don't you want to be like me?" You would probably say, "No, thanks." And I'd say, "But I'm an example of the Gospel." And you'd say, "No, no, no, no."

When I walk in here in a suit, anointed of God, I'm saying, "Hey, I've got something to share with you, something good's going to happen to you. Get your Bible. We're going to get blessed today. We're going to get anointed and get our needs met." Does that sound a little better than the other? Now if you have to go the other way, which, at times I have had to, then you can do it.

There are a lot of lies about this man Jesus. He

was somebody. He wore a special, one-of-a-kind, seamless robe so costly that at His crucifixion they gambled for who could get possession of it. He didn't go around dressed like a hobo, half starving, but He was willing to obey the Father no matter the cost. Why? Because there were believers *"who ministered unto him of their substance" (Luke 8:3).* Paul said, *"But I have all, and abound: I am full, having received of Epaphroditus."* Having received. Paul said, *"I am full, having received of Epaphroditus the things which were sent from you."* And here's how the Apostle described the way God saw it: *"An odor of a sweet smell, a sacrifice acceptable, well-pleasing to God."* Notice the first one, an odor of a sweet smell. That's what we call sweet-smelling money. I want you to know how God feels when we don't get into giving and receiving. It's not sweet-smelling money; instead it's got a bad odor. It takes your breath away. It tears up the kingdom. You know, this sounds kind of funny, but you want to cry.

An Acceptable Sacrifice

The first two boys born were Cain and Abel. And Abel made his sacrifice by faith and was accepted. Cain made his sacrifice without faith and was not accepted, and he got mad and killed Abel . . . the first murder in the world. His sacrifice was not acceptable. Get into giving and receiving, giving and receiving, receiving and giving, because your sacrifice is not acceptable without faith. By itself, your giving does not have an odor of a sweet smell to God. You're never going to make a sacrifice acceptable to God by giving alone. You must combine it with your faith.

Remember what I said in the beginning of this

chapter about the cat-seller and the antique dealer? The old antique dealer thought he would steal that antique from that merchant, but the merchant got to him because he sold him a cat using the best cat-seller he ever had. Do you get the point? It won't work to try to fool God regarding your tithes and offerings. You can't put one over on God. In *Galatians 6:7* it says, *"Be not deceived; God is not mocked: for whatsoever a man soweth, that shall he also reap."*

Paul said to the Philippians, "You're the only ones." If we want to please God with our faith and honor God with our seed — then we must stop TALKING Seed-Faith and begin LIVING Seed-Faith. Get into total receiving and total giving. Make your seed send out a sweet smell. Let God take the acceptable sacrifice, and attach your faith to it to make it well-pleasing to Him. *Hebrews 11:6,* *"Without faith, it is impossible to please him* [God]: *for . . . he is a <u>rewarder</u> of them that diligently seek him."* A what? A rewarder. God is a rewarder of everything good that we do in faith.

Your Part and God's Part

The moment you do something from your heart and with your faith, then you have a Bible right to expect the seed of an equivalent benefit: For every action, there is an equal reaction. God is just like that. When you do your part of what God tells you in His Word, God is obligated to do His part of the Word. The Bible contains a series of if/then clauses. If you do this, then God will do this. So, when you do your part, God will do His part. He has to, He's held by His Word to do so, and God is not a man that He should lie. (See *Numbers 23:19.*) When you give to God expect to receive, but not from people.

People are not our source. About the time we begin to look to people, they begin to let us down. But God will not let you down. He won't desert you. He said He'd never leave us or forsake us.

Now let's look at verse 19. We get to the great verse. Think of the Apostle Paul here. He says, "I've gone through all of it for you, Philippian believers, you've been doing what this says. Now that you've done your part, I have the privilege of telling you what God will do as His part, and I can say, *'But my God shall supply all your need according to his riches in glory by Christ Jesus.'* God didn't say He would supply half your needs. He said He'd supply *all* your needs. And it's going to work. It has to work because you've done your part and you've believed God and believed His Word."

Listen friend, if we do what God said in His Word, it's going to work. The "well-pleasing sacrifice" to God is shown in the miracles and the signs and wonders and the healings and the supplying of our needs. This message from the Apostle Paul to the giving and receiving group at Philippi, all comes down to one thing . . . making God the SOURCE OF YOUR TOTAL SUPPLY, spiritually, physically, and yes, even financially. It's not sacrilegious to believe God to supply your needs according to His riches in glory by Christ Jesus. It's the Bible!

Make Him your **PHYSICAL SOURCE.**
Make Him your **FINANCIAL SOURCE.**
   And, above ALL,
Make Him your **SPIRITUAL SOURCE.**

THE SOURCE OF YOUR TOTAL SUPPLY.

CHAPTER 8

KAREN:
"I HAD $15 LEFT AND GAVE
$10 OF IT TO GOD."

I got saved back in 1982. I was selling drugs. I was an alcoholic, and when I got saved, I got totally delivered from all that. In fact, to look at a bottle of beer makes me nauseous now. But I was out of work. I had lost my job. I was a hothead. I tried to buy a business and lost that, too. That's what brought me to the Lord. I was continually at the bottom. The girl across the street from me had been saved, and she came over and said to me, "You wouldn't believe what I found. His Name is Jesus." Three weeks later I got saved.

I can remember the day that I just happened to flip on the television and I saw Richard Roberts on TV. The only thing I knew about Richard Roberts was that he was Oral Roberts' son. I didn't know anything else about him. He was singing "God Is Not Through Blessing You." I just sat there and listened to him.

He was talking about Seed-Faith giving and I

had no idea what that was. I thought, this sounds crazy, because he said, "Sow a seed of faith to God and He'll multiply that." I was just beginning to learn how to read the Bible, and I hadn't gotten to that part. I was just getting into tithing. I thought, I don't even have a job. What's he talking about here? But he was saying if you give — if you let go of what's in your hand toward God — then God will let go of what is in His hand toward you. And for some reason, the rest of that day I kept thinking about that. Well, he got it from the Bible, he gave Scriptures to prove it. It's got to be right. So I started sending seed to the ministry.

It seemed that after I sent in my Seed-Faith, somebody would fill up my gas tank or give me extra work. Things were happening that hadn't happened before. I was smart enough to realize that maybe it was because I let go of something that was in my hand and God was sending it back to me. It was always more than what I sent in. I finally realized that's what Richard was talking about — Seed-Faith giving and receiving.

After I started tithing to my church, the Lord gave me various ministries to give to, but Oral and Richard Roberts were the very first ministry. God laid it on my heart to support them and I intend to be faithful. There's been an abundance because I'm a Seed-Faith giver and receiver. When I sow a seed of faith, I just let it go and I say, "God, I'm not going to ask You for something You've already promised me. So here it is. Thank You for the harvest." I've been Seed-Faith giving for nine years and it's a regular rhythm now. It's just giving and receiving. I just do it, I don't even think about it anymore. I'm not afraid because God has proven Himself in my life.

Recently I turned on the TV and heard Oral saying, "If you really want God to bless you, I have a book here that can really help you." He was giving it away free, postage paid, so I called the Abundant Life Prayer Group to request it. When I got it, I read it all in one night.

I like to prove things by the Scripture, so I tested him on this. I looked up everything Oral said and I could not find anything wrong in his book. It's totally Bible. So, I started following the principles in it and jobs started coming in. Raises were coming in and I'm talking about raises of $100 or $125 a week. I can't explain it, but whenever God says sow, I get excited because there's something special on the end of it.

I know I am where I'm at today because of the Bible teaching on Seed-Faith giving. God does honor His Word, all you have to do is test Him, just prove Him. He said, *"Prove me . . . if I will not open you the windows of heaven and pour you out a blessing" (Malachi 3:10).* And I found out that is exactly what He does.

I asked the Lord, "What amount should I sow to get the money I need for Bible school?" And He spoke to me very clearly, "$10." I immediately filled out the prayer request form, wrote on it that I needed $800 and sent it to Oral Roberts for the work of the Gospel. It was at a time when I wasn't working. All I had was $15 and a car payment coming up. Well, $10 was two-thirds of it. It was a very big amount to me.

And the Lord showed me in His Word *(Mark 12:41-44)* where He was sitting by the Temple treasury, and the rich men came in and put in huge offerings, then along comes this little widow woman. She put in two mites because that was all

81

she had. And Jesus said that she gave **more** than all the rest because she gave all she had to live on at that time. To Jesus that meant more than all that huge amount of the rich people. To Jesus it was the attitude of the heart that was important. The widow gave her two mites as her seed for a miracle. She proved God, and I'm sure she got her miracle.

When you just have $15 and you give $10 of it to God, that's a lot. Immediately after you let go of the $10, you've dropped it in the mailbox, it's like the devil's right there saying, "Well, you've only got $5 left. That was stupid." The first time you ever do that you want to crawl into that mailbox, and go get your $10 back. All the way home I had the harassment from the devil, "That was dumb. You only got $5 left." But within 20 minutes somebody had filled up my gas tank. I had an empty gas tank, and somebody came along and filled it up.

Just two months later, my brother called. He had been on alcohol and was a drug addict for 18 straight years. He had lost his daughter, his marriage, everything. He said, "I don't know what you've got, but I'm at the end of my rope and I need what you have. Can I go to church with you?" And I said, "You sure can." It just so happened that Sunday that Dwight Thompson preached about the prodigal son. When he gave the altar call my brother actually knocked down the cameraman getting to the altar. My brother had come to church with withdrawal symptoms because he tried to stop using drugs himself. The sweat was just pouring off him, and he was shaking. He knelt down to receive the Lord, and when he got up the sweat was gone. He had stopped shaking and within 48 hours, all his withdrawal symptoms were gone. Within only

90 days he went back for drug tests. All symptoms were gone from his body. It looked like he had never even been on drugs.

One night he called me over to his house and he said, "Here, the Lord told me to give you this," and it was $800. "Here, go to Bible school." I had seeded specifically for that $800. I seeded for a specific harvest. I told the Lord, "I'm giving this $10 believing that I have received my money to attend Bible school, according to *Mark 11:22-24*." I didn't ask Him about it. I just continued to thank Him for it every day. I said, "I know, Lord, You promised to multiply my seed, so I believe I receive my harvest according to *Mark 11:22-24*." And it showed up two months later. It showed up in an unexpected way, but when you think you've got God down pat, He'll come to you another way. I love the way He does it.

At the time, I thought you had to plant a big seed to get a big harvest, but I found out that God just wants you to be faithful. If you just sow that seed, He'll multiply it back, especially if He lays it on your heart to sow a specific amount. After I've sown a seed, the letters I get from Oral or Richard will quote a Scripture or several Scriptures that are exactly what God has told me just maybe days before.

I decided to prove God — to find out if Seed-Faith was a gimmick or if it really was of God. And I found out it's no gimmick. To me, proving God is taking Him at His Word. I dared to prove God and I found out He's absolutely true to His Word every time. He's faithful to His Word. He's never failed me. To me, that's proving God.

I love Lindsay, and her book, *36 Hours With An Angel*. If anybody has ever been hurt as far as losing, it's Lindsay. I don't think I could go through what she's been through. She had two miscarriages and a tumor, and then she had little Richard Oral and he died. By the time I got to that part in her book, I was thinking, I can't believe she's still got her sanity. But now she and Richard have three little girls. It's like the bottom had fallen out of her life but then God built a floor. That's what's getting me through my life right now and the things I'm going through. This book came the exact time I needed it. I've read this a dozen times over and over, and this book has encouraged me to believe that God is going to restore to me all that I've lost.

I also received a letter from Lindsay saying, "Don't give up." And that came at a time when I was ready to give up. I still read her book. I would recommend it to anybody that's had a loss of any kind, because she knows. She's been through it, and there's nothing like reading a testimony of someone who's been through it. Anybody can say, "Yeah, I know how you feel," but if you haven't been through it, you can't really know. This is a book for people who have had loss of any kind, really, because God just doesn't restore people, God is a multiplying God. He's not a dividing God. He's not a subtracting God. He's a multiplying God.

Make Him your **PHYSICAL SOURCE.**
Make Him your **FINANCIAL SOURCE.**
And, above ALL,
Make Him your **SPIRITUAL SOURCE.**

THE SOURCE OF YOUR TOTAL SUPPLY.

NOTE: To receive your copy of *36 Hours With An Angel* by Lindsay, send in the request form in the back of this book.

III. GOD IS THE SOURCE OF YOUR SPIRITUAL SUPPLY

CHAPTER 9

THE DEVIL WANTS US TO BACKSLIDE UNTIL WE SLIDE RIGHT OUT OF OUR FAITH

"The just shall live by faith."

FOUR TIMES THE BIBLE SAYS "THE JUST SHALL LIVE BY FAITH."

#1 **HABAKKUK 2:4** - *Behold, his soul which is lifted up is not upright in him: but **the just shall live by his faith.***

#2 **ROMANS 1:17** - *For therein is the righteousness of God revealed from faith to faith: as it is written. **The just shall live by faith.***

#3 **GALATIANS 3:11** - *But that no man is justified by the law in the sight of God, it is evident: for, **the just shall live by faith.***

#4 **HEBREWS 10:38** - ***Now the just shall live by faith:** but if any man draw back, my soul shall have no pleasure in him.*

Our Faith Pleases God
Look carefully at the last part of *Hebrews 10:38,*

"If any man draw back, my soul shall have no plea-sure in him." Just how important is our faith? Take a look at *Hebrews 11:6, ". . .without faith it is impossible to please him* [God]." Our faith pleases God. Our lack of faith displeases God.

Isn't it awesome to know that we don't have to wonder how to please God? He tells us it is our faith that pleases Him. He always loves us, but the only time He takes pleasure in us is when we touch Him with our faith, for without faith it is impossible to please Him. Sometimes we spend a lot of time and worry trying to figure out how to please other people. But we can know exactly how to please God . . . it's by faith. We serve a miracle-working God and we can touch Him with our faith.

No wonder the devil schemes to rob us of our faith — because without it we can't please God. No wonder his purpose is to steal, kill, and destroy. (See *John 10:10*.) If the devil can steal your faith, he's stolen your pleasure with God and God's plea-sure with you. Now wouldn't that just delight the devil. Your faith is a TOP priority with God <u>and</u> with the devil. And that's why it needs to be <u>your</u> top priority. It's vital that we *"fight the good fight of faith"* according to *I Timothy 6:12*. And it's very important when we put on the whole armor of God, according to *Ephesians 6:11-18*, ABOVE ALL, we take the shield of faith so we will be able to quench the fiery darts of the wicked.

Faith Comes by Hearing
and Hearing by the Word of God

Hebrews 11:1 describes our faith as the sub-stance of things hoped for, the evidence of things not seen. I think we often doubt our own faith and, therefore, begin to doubt God, because faith is in the invisible, unseen realm. In the supernatural, miraculous realm of God, faith is our provision so we can believe in a God we cannot physically see. Yet, through the eyes of our spirit, we not only can see Him, we can touch Him with our faith!

Don't Weary or Give Up

Today we live in what I call a "microwave society." We want all our needs met in an instant. It's like instant breakfast, instant potatoes, instant coffee. Everything is done for us with a push of a button at our fingertips. And, although I've seen some instantaneous miracles, God doesn't <u>always</u> work that way, even though many times we'd like for Him to. Keep in mind *Galatians 6:9, "Let us not be weary in well doing: for in due season we shall reap, if we faint not."*

You know, I've heard pregnant women around the fifth or sixth month say, "I wish I'd have this baby today." Well, deep in their hearts, they don't really mean that, that's just their weariness talking. Deep in their hearts they want that precious little baby born in its "due season," which is nine months. Anything short of that could be dangerous. And friend, in the same way, it's always dangerous to be weary concerning God's timetable, because He said we'd reap in due season if we do not give up.

One way to keep going and finish what God tells us to do is "by not being weary" and by not losing faith. Paul said in *II Timothy 4:7, "I have finished my course, I have kept the faith."* The only way he could finish is to <u>keep the faith.</u>

Meditate on the Word

HOW DO YOU KEEP FAITH in the midst of the fiery furnace — in the difficulties and struggles you face, in the pressures of your life? *Psalm 1:1-3* says *"Blessed is the man that walketh not in the counsel of the ungodly, nor standeth in the way of sinners, nor sitteth in the seat of the scornful. But his delight is in the law of the Lord; and in his law doth he meditate day and night. And he shall be like a tree planted by the rivers of water, that bringeth forth his fruit in his season; his leaf also shall not wither; and whatsoever he doeth shall prosper."*

To keep our faith, we <u>must</u> meditate night and day on God's Word, not on the words of the ungodly world, but meditate on God's Word. The more we learn God's laws and do what His Word says, the more we will begin to prosper. We need to find out what God's Word says about our situation and act on His Word.

Remember *Romans 10:17* says, *"Faith cometh by hearing, and hearing by the word of God."* Let's go to the story of the fiery furnace in the Word of God and see what happened when God moved in on the scene in the third chapter of the Book of Daniel.

The Babylonian King Nebuchadnezzar built a golden image to himself and commanded that at the sound of the *"cornet, flute, harp, sackbut, psaltery, and dulcimer, and all kinds of music, ye fall down and worship the golden image" (Daniel 3:15).* The Hebrew princes, Shadrach, Meshach, and Abednego, refused to bow to any other God, but to their God only — the God of Abraham, Isaac, and Jacob. This was reported to the king and immediately he sent for them — giving them one more chance to bow to his golden idol or be cast into his fiery furnace.

Refusing to give in to the threats of Nebuchadnezzar, Shadrach, Meshach and Abednego said, "We may burn, but we won't bow."

The angry king finally succeeded in having them thrown fully clothed into the burning fiery furnace and stood by waiting for the fire to consume the three young Hebrew men who wouldn't bow.

Faith in Life's Fiery Furnaces

How real the fiery furnaces of life are today. Many of God's people have been thrown into fiery furnaces heated seven times hotter than normal. Perhaps you wouldn't bow and you have been thrust into the furnace for your testimony, your integrity and conviction. Or, perhaps you have even had some of your dearest friendships betrayed. I know how hot that furnace is, for I, too, have had many of my friendships betrayed. Some of my friends have given me no reason, but have simply turned their backs and walked away. I know of no furnace hotter than the loss of friendship.

Sometimes the fiery furnace that opens its burning mouth to sear us is financial setback and material loss. But friend, don't ever forget what happened in that furnace.

When King Nebuchadnezzar's soldiers threw those boys into the furnace, the Fourth Man hurled himself through space, and in a moment's time was beside them, going into the burning fiery furnace with them. By the time the door was shut He had ripped off their bonds and clothed them with divine protection. When the king looked in, all four of them were walking around in the fire, unhurt and untouched by the flames. Even the king had to recognize the miracle and proclaim, *"The form of the fourth man is like the Son of God!"* (See *Daniel 3:25.*)

From Genesis through Revelation, the Bible describes Who the Fourth Man is. The Fourth Man

91

is God, <u>our Source, in whatever form we need Him to be.</u>

Who is this Fourth Man?

In Genesis He is the *Seed of the Woman.*

In Exodus He is the *Passover Lamb.*

In Leviticus He is our *High Priest.*

In Numbers He is the *Pillar of Cloud* by day and the *Pillar of Fire* by night.

In Deuteronomy He is the *Prophet like unto Moses.*

In Joshua He is the *Captain of our Salvation.*

In Judges He is our *Judge and Lawgiver.*

In Ruth He is our *Kinsman-Redeemer.*

In I and II Samuel He is our *Trusted Prophet.*

In I and II Kings and I and II Chronicles He is our *Reigning King.*

In Ezra He is our *Faithful Scribe.*

In Nehemiah He is the *Rebuilder of the Broken Down Walls* of human life.

In Esther He is our *Mordecai.*

In Job He is our *Ever-Living Redeemer,* "For I know my Redeemer liveth."

Who is this Fourth Man?

In Psalms He is our *Shepherd.*

In Proverbs and Ecclesiastes He is our *Wisdom.*

In the Song of Solomon He is our *Lover and Bridegroom.*

In Isaiah He is the *Prince of Peace.*

In Jeremiah He is the *Righteous Branch.*

In Lamentations He is our *Weeping Prophet.*

In Ezekiel He is the *Wonderful Four-Faced Man.*

And in Daniel He is the *Fourth Man in Life's Fiery Furnaces.*

Who is this Fourth Man?

In Hosea He is the *Faithful Husband,* forever married to the backslider.

In Joel He is the *Baptizer with the Holy Ghost and Fire.*

In Amos He is our *Burden-Bearer.*

In Obadiah He is the *Mighty to Save.*

In Jonah He is our great *Foreign Missionary.*

In Micah He is the *Messenger with Beautiful Feet.*

In Nahum He is the *Avenger of God's Elect.*

In Habakkuk He is *God's Evangelist,* crying, "Revive thy work in the midst of the years."

In Zephaniah He is our *Savior.*

In Haggai He is the *Restorer of God's Lost Heritage.*

In Zechariah He is the *Fountain Opened in the House of David* for sin and uncleanness.

In Malachi He is the *Sun of Righteousness,* rising with healing in His wings.

Who is this Fourth Man?

In Matthew He is the *Messiah.*

In Mark He is the *Wonder-Worker.*

In Luke He is the *Son of Man.*

In John He is the *Son of God.*

In Acts He is the *Holy Ghost.*

In Romans He is our *Justifier.*

In I and II Corinthians He is our *Sanctifier.*

In Galatians He is the *Redeemer from the Curse of the Law.*

In Ephesians He is the *Christ of Unsearchable Riches.*

In Philippians He is the *God Who Supplies All Our Needs.*

In Colossians He is the *Fullness of the Godhead Bodily.*

In I and II Thessalonians He is our *Soon-Coming King.*

In I and II Timothy He is our *Mediator Between God and Man.*

In Titus He is our *Faithful Pastor.*

In Philemon He is the *Friend That Sticketh Closer than a Brother.*

Who is this Fourth Man?

In Hebrews He is the *Blood of the Everlasting Covenant.*

In James He is our *Great Physician,* for "The prayer of faith shall save the sick."

In I and II Peter He is our *Chief Shepherd,* who soon shall appear with a crown of unfading glory.

In I, II and III John He is *Love.*

In Jude He is the *Lord Coming with Ten Thousands of His Saints.*

And in Revelation He is the *KING OF KINGS AND LORD OF LORDS!*

Who is this Fourth Man?

He is Abel's Sacrifice, Noah's Rainbow, Abraham's Ram, Isaac's Wells, Jacob's Ladder, Moses' Rod, Joshua's Sun and Moon that stood still, Elijah's Mantle, Elisha's Staff, Gideon's Fleece, Samuel's Horn of Oil, David's Slingshot, Isaiah's Fig Poultice, Hezekiah's Sundial, Daniel's Visions, Amos' Burden and Malachi's Sun of Righteousness.

Who is this Fourth Man?

He is Peter's Shadow, Stephen's Signs and Wonders, Paul's Handkerchiefs and Aprons, and John's Pearly White City.

Who is this Fourth Man?

He is a *Father to the Orphan, Husband to the Widow,* to the traveler in the night He is the *Bright and Morning Star;* to those who walk in the lonesome valley He is the *Lily of the Valley,* the *Rose of Sharon* and *Honey in the Rock.* He is the *Brightness of God's Glory,* the *Express Image of His Person,* the *King of Glory,* the *Pearl of Great Price,* the *Rock in a Weary Land,* the *Cup that Runneth Over,* the *Rod and Staff* that comfort. And the government of our lives is upon His shoulders.

Who is this Fourth Man?

He is Jesus of Nazareth, the Son of the living God! Your Savior! Your Companion! Your Lord and King!

YOUR SOURCE OF TOTAL SUPPLY!

I'm stirred in my soul, my inner man, the core of my being to tell you today, don't be tricked by the lies of the devil! Don't listen to the accusations of the great accuser when he comes at you with his evil lies! Don't let the devil steal your faith today! For God has a supply for you, for your life. Don't give up — reach up in faith to that Fourth Man, the Source of your health and prosperity in all your life.

Make Him your **PHYSICAL SOURCE.**
Make Him your **FINANCIAL SOURCE.**
And, above ALL,
Make Him your **SPIRITUAL SOURCE.**

THE SOURCE OF YOUR TOTAL SUPPLY.

CHAPTER 10

PASTOR RESCUES CHILDREN FROM FIRE

Here in Tulsa, Billy Joe Daugherty, an ORU graduate, founder and pastor of one of the largest churches in America, Victory Christian Center, experienced the devil's fiery furnace, not only spiritually, but literally when their house caught fire in the middle of the night. Although he was able to get his wife Sharon and two children, Sarah and John, out of the house, he soon realized his other two children were still in the house. Instantly, he went back into the house looking for Ruth and Paul.

Billy Joe didn't let anything get in his path. He had a certain point of destination and that was the location of Ruth and Paul. Regardless of the billowing smoke and the inability to see anything but a black cloud in his face — he didn't let any obstacle get in his way. Yes, there was a fire; yes, there was smoke; yes, it was absolutely impossible to see; and, yes, it was at great personal risk. But none of the circumstances got in his way to rescue Ruth and Paul from their burning home. Running back into the burning, smoke-filled house, choking and calling for little Ruth and Paul, Billy Joe found Ruth first and pulled her out. Then he ran back inside a second time and found six-year-old Paul in the hallway, dazed and unable to find his way out.

In what could have been a horrible tragedy, the whole family got safely outside the burning house. Billy Joe suffered for a few days with smoke inhalation and second degree burns, but was determined by God's help to get his voice back and preach in his church the following Sunday.

As someone once said, "These are the times that try men's souls." But Billy Joe and Sharon know that <u>God is the Source of their total supply.</u> They learned that while attending Oral Roberts University, and they live by it every day. It is not just something they say, it is a vital, living reality to them. God comes through for them when tragedy comes.

Billy Joe did preach in his church the following Sunday after their fire. He could only whisper at the time, but he proclaimed the Word of God and gave God glory for saving his family.

He said while telling the story to his congregation that he never wanted to go to hell — "The smell and taste of fire and smoke here were enough to last a lifetime." Billy Joe also said, "We are not considering the things we lost in the fire. Material things are not very important to us. What is important are the lives of our family."

What the devil meant for evil, God turned around for good, for Billy Joe was able to bring peo-

The Daugherty family offered a prayer of thanksgiving in their church.

ple to a saving knowledge of Jesus Christ as he told the story of their disaster.

Billy Joe told me later he realized that the Source of his total supply — the Fourth Man — was in the fiery furnace with him. And as a miracle God saved Shadrach, Meshach, and Abednego, He saved Billy Joe and his family. Miraculous deliverance — that is what happened, and it can happen for you if you believe and know that God is your Source.

Make Him your **PHYSICAL SOURCE.**
Make Him your **FINANCIAL SOURCE.**
    And, above ALL,
Make Him your **SPIRITUAL SOURCE.**

THE SOURCE OF YOUR TOTAL SUPPLY

CHAPTER 11

CAROL:
FROM DRUGS
TO DELIVERANCE

Carol Cichelli had been under the bondage of drugs and alcohol for years. As a young person, she knew what it was like to have the devil in control. Her testimony so touched my heart that I believe it will stir your soul with a knowledge of Who God is and what He can do for you. We often sing, "It is no secret what God can do. What He's done for others, He'll do for you." I really believe what God did for others and for the Carol Cichellis of the world, He can do for you when you make Him the Source of your spiritual supply. Read her testimony with the ears of your soul tuned in . . .

My precious years, from ages 18 to 30, were stolen from me because of drugs and alcohol. My drinking problem got worse and worse as time went on, and after awhile alcohol didn't agree with me so I switched to drugs. With drugs I got a much higher high and eventually I started to steal to get more drugs. At one time, I had three or four doctors' prescriptions going. Then, all this came to a screeching halt when I was hit by a car in a very serious hit-and-run accident. I was knocked out and dragged about 30 feet. I was in the hospital for six weeks and during that time I cried out to the Lord. This is when *I began calling the Prayer Tower* and I believe their prayers had a lot to do with my deliverance.

After the accident, I reached out for help for my heavy drug use. One Sunday in my room at a rehabilitation hospital where I was recovering from the drugs, I was watching Oral Roberts on television. I will never forget that. Even in the state I was in, I will never forget how I felt the power of Jesus through Oral Roberts so strongly that I began to weep right there in the hospital. I just felt like the Lord walked into that room. I felt the power of God come through that TV and it really went into me. That made an impact on me and even though I was still struggling with taking drugs, I continued to call the Prayer Tower. They helped me and prayed with me and through that, I began to recover. God took control and began to take me out of that situation. I have been sober and drug free ever since, and that was 16 years ago!

Now, notice two very important things about Carol's testimony:

#1 — She felt that the devil had actually stolen her youthful years away from her. There are people today who have lost a part of their lives. The devil has literally stolen what they have.

#2 — Second, she allowed me to be what I am: A prophet of God's healing power. She listened to what I had to say. I believe God has given me something to say to people today who have lost a portion of their lives. You may be physically alive, but you feel like you're dead on the inside. You're like living, walking death. Or, perhaps the devil has actually stolen a

part of your life through drugs or alcohol or in some other way. I believe I have a message for you today that will really help establish you. And it's this: In II Chronicles 20:20 it says, "Believe God and so shall you be established; believe his prophets and so shall you prosper." What God is saying to you here is that ONLY by believing Him will your life be truly ESTABLISHED. And, by believing His prophets, so shall you prosper.

Don't let something that has been stolen out of your life get you down to where you don't believe the Lord, and He can't <u>establish</u> you anymore. I want you to believe that God has prophets on this earth, men and women who carry God's prophetic spirit in their lives and speak His words, and who can pray a powerful prayer that can supernaturally be used of God to change your life. The message to you is that God is a good God and He sent His Son Jesus Christ of Nazareth for healing, delivering, saving miracles for you and me today. If you hear that a few ministers whom you trust, have sinned or made a big mistake, remember the vast majority are living clean, productive lives before God and through them you can believe the Scriptures and prosper. They are sent from God to help you get your needs met — to help get back what satan has stolen from you.

Don't give up. "Believe in the Lord your God, so shall you be established; believe his prophets so shall you prosper" (II Chronicles 20:20).

Make Him your **PHYSICAL SOURCE.**
Make Him your **FINANCIAL SOURCE.**
And, above ALL,

Make Him your **SPIRITUAL SOURCE.**

THE SOURCE OF YOUR TOTAL SUPPLY.

CHAPTER 12

RICK AND KIMBERLY:
AND NOW . . .
"RICHARD ROBERTS LIVE"

One young couple that got tuned in to God, their Source, is a man and woman from Suwannee, Georgia, named Rick and Kimberly Jecker. The devil, the accuser, had so deceived them that it looked like it was all over for them, spiritually, financially, and especially emotionally. Marijuana, cocaine and alcohol had become the source for their lives. *But when the substances could no longer sustain them, their source ran out. As they were about to hit bottom, they rediscovered their* <u>Source</u> *for their lives. While watching Richard and Lindsay on their daily television program, Kimberly got connected to God, her Source of total supply. . . and the miracles began.*

RICK: My wife and I had been saved in the past, but we had backslidden. Marijuana, cocaine, and alcohol had become the focal point of our lives, but we found they didn't solve any of our problems. The term "household salvation" meant nothing to my wife and me, but it did to our family members who were praying for our deliverance. The Lord was dealing with our hearts to come back to Him. Finally, we had enough. We repented and accepted Jesus as our Savior and immediately our lifestyle began changing. We started watching your program and we saw such joy there! Your words were full of faith that really began feeding us.

KIMBERLY: One day I turned on the television and I said, "No soap operas, no more talk shows, none of this garbage." I started flipping through the channels and I got "Richard Roberts Live." I'm thinking to myself, I'm going to sit down and check this out. At that time, I didn't have a church. And so I'm watching this guy and I'm thinking, Lord, bless his heart. I think really that I had faith, but it was like it was just steadily growing.

I began feeding on this message by Richard. One of the first things that he said was, "You're not worthless. You're not worthless." And that hit home, because for so many years I had allowed the devil to convince me that I was of no value. But I knew after I heard that, that there was victory for me. There was genuine victory. The Lord loved me so much, I sat down and watched this man and woman of God and I knew in my heart by the Scriptures that they quoted that God definitely has a place for me with Him. Richard and Lindsay's ministry has shown us that God loves us and we are of value to Him. In their daily TV program, they've helped us to find our place in Him, a Source we can trust with all of our lives.

If God did this for Rick and Kimberly, He can deliver you. Your problem may be different from theirs, but our God is a big God. He loves you and He is able to deliver you.

Make Him your **PHYSICAL SOURCE.**
Make Him your **FINANCIAL SOURCE.**
   And, above ALL,
Make Him your **SPIRITUAL SOURCE.**

THE SOURCE OF YOUR TOTAL SUPPLY.

CHAPTER 13

VANTRICE: THE WOMAN WHO GOT IT ALL

One of the best testimonies that demonstrates III John 2 came to me from a lady in New Mexico named Vantrice Burkes. From the "bottom of the spiritual barrel," Vantrice came to one of our seminars on the campus of Oral Roberts University. We have followed her life from a virtually hopeless human being to her discovery of God as the Source of her spiritual supply, and becoming a preacher on fire for God. From a tiny seed of beginnings to having her needs abundantly met, Vantrice demonstrates the end results of making God the Source of her financial supply. Recently, we heard again from Vantrice. God has seen her through a series of miracles following a near-fatal stroke that became a glorious healing as she made God the Source of her physical supply. Vantrice is a living, walking miracle that powerfully exemplifies III John 2 — <u>MAKING GOD THE SOURCE OF HER TOTAL SUPPLY</u> in every area

*of her life, physically, financially and spiritually. I
encourage you to absorb every word of her testimony
into your soul like a spiritual sponge. Drink her
words into your spirit today and let her words
encourage you to focus on God as your Source.*

An alcoholic roars through the lives of others
like a tornado. I was an alcoholic for fifteen years,
but I never thought of myself as a bad person. I was
a very sick person. My husband was an alcoholic at
the same time. I ran over him a couple of times
with the car, shot at him, we had brawls, fights,
and constant revolving poverty because alcoholics
don't handle their affairs too well.

I had been drunk off and on for about three
months, and I was lying on the couch, when a
friend came in and threw the book, *Miracle of Seed-
Faith* by Oral Roberts, down on the coffee table.
She said, "Read this. I don't think there's any hope
for you, but read it anyway." I read it and it
impressed me so much, that I went out and picked
up pop bottles and aluminum beer cans to get five
dollars to send to Oral for his ministry. When I sent
it, I wrote him a letter with that little seed, and
poured out my heart. I talked to him in my letter
like we were face to face.

I'd been raised in a church where it was hellfire
and damnation and God's "gonna get you." I
thought they were a bunch of Christian bounty
hunters getting a prize for how many they could
send to hell. All they ever told me is that I was
going to hell. I knew that . . . I was already in hell. I
just needed a way out.

Nobody ever told me that Jesus loved me or that
there was a way out. They just said, "You're going
to hell if you don't quit this." Nobody told me how to
quit. So when I wrote Oral that letter, he wrote

back and said, "That's okay. Jesus loves you just exactly like you are today. I'm going to pray." I carried that letter around with me until it literally disintegrated.

Oral's *Miracle of Seed-Faith* book helped me, too. There were Scriptures like *"Give and it shall be given to you" (Luke 6:38)*. It also said if you tithe, God will open the windows of Heaven and pour you out a blessing there's not room enough to receive, and He will rebuke the devourer for your sake. (See *Malachi 3:10,11*.) The book also said that Jesus said He came to heal the brokenhearted, set the captives free, and set at liberty those that had been bruised. (See *Luke 4:18*.) My seed of faith was my connection to all the promises in the Bible. Oral kept writing to me, telling me that God is a good God, and I kept sending in my Seed-Faith. That was 20 years ago.

At that time in my life, there was nothing in the house to feed the kids, and all the utilities were turned off. We had a marriage where we were fighting and brawling all the time. A lot of people are going through that right now. No <u>human</u> power can relieve your alcoholism, but God can and will if you seek Him. The first thing you do is <u>turn to God</u>.

I went into full-time ministry 16 years ago because I wanted to help people who'd been where I was. Nobody has to live that way. Family problems, relationship problems, financial problems, there is a way out. Now I have a retreat center. People come here and stay for four days to meet Jesus. The most basic thing they need is Jesus. And I always give them a copy of Oral's book, *Miracle of Seed-Faith*. It helped me. It will help them. I love the Scripture, *III John 2*, that Oral always quotes that says, *"Beloved, I wish above all things that you will pros-*

per and be in health, even as your soul prospers."
That's peace. No matter what is going on, I have
peace.

In the midst of ministry and all that God was
doing, I had a massive stroke. My husband drove
me to the emergency room. I was then transported
to another hospital and I heard the doctor tell my
husband and son that I may not make it till morning. But I was so peaceful. I was trying to get
enough reason to fight it. I could feel myself going,
but I was just so peaceful.

I was completely paralyzed on my right side. I
couldn't talk, couldn't move, couldn't turn over,
couldn't feed myself, couldn't do anything. I was
just laying there helpless, and I remembered what
Oral had said at the seminars. "If you can just
move a toe, do it." So I did. I would scoot down in
the bed, get my feet against the foot board, and I
would get hold of my hand and move it. I was determined to make it move.

My son turned on the TV in the hospital room,
and it was one of the nights that Richard and
Lindsay were hosting the Trinity Broadcasting
Network show. I've become such close friends with
Richard and Lindsay both. I recognized their voic-
es.

It was so wonderful – but it wouldn't have
worked with just Richard's voice. I needed both of
them. Richard was the spiritual, and Lindsay was
the tender. I needed both of them that night. It was
their voices that pulled me back so God could start
the healing.

Within ten minutes, I was opening my eyes and
trying to communicate with my son. You see,
Richard and Lindsay and I have a well-established
friendship of long-standing. When the crisis time

came, I recognized their voices. It's the same thing with Jesus. If we get our relationship established with Him, when the crisis time comes, we'll recognize His voice.

I was in the hospital for ten days. I expected instant healing. It had always been that way. Even after surgery, I never was sick for more than a week, but with this I had to go through the process of recovery, and the feelings and fears that you had to fight. Then satan would come in with, "What if? What if?" My job is giving people hope and faith, and then I had to practice it for me.

But we have a saying. When satan tells you you're going under, we say, "Oh, yeah? Well, watch this. It's Red Sea time." It didn't scare me. The doctor had said, "I don't know if she'll make it till morning." I kept thinking, well, I've always made it. I've always made it. If I made it when I was wiped-out drunk, driving a car a hundred miles an hour the wrong way on the freeway in California, with big cliffs down to the ocean, and God saved me from that, something like this ought to be a snap for Him. It didn't scare me.

I went from paralyzed, to a wheelchair, to a walker, to a cane, and now I'm walking. Even though it wasn't instant, it's still a miracle, because I was told I would never walk again. What people need to realize is that just because it's not an instant miracle, God's healing power is still at work. I remember Oral saying that sometimes the gradual healings are the ones that last. This one's going to last.

Because Oral reached out to me and told me Jesus loved me, and God is a good God, I was set free from alcohol and drugs, my marriage was healed, my family's been restored, and the finances were restored. My body's been healed from a massive stroke and God has turned my hurts into healing for other people. Oral said one time, "Sometimes it's people who've been broken by life and put back together by Jesus who really know how to help other broken people." Well, that qualifies me. Jesus turned my hurts into healing for others, and I sure have learned how to help hurting people.

Make Him your **PHYSICAL SOURCE.**
Make Him your **FINANCIAL SOURCE.**
    And, above ALL,
Make Him your **SPIRITUAL SOURCE.**

THE SOURCE OF YOUR TOTAL SUPPLY.

NOTE: See page 119 for your copy of *Miracle of Seed-Faith* by Oral Roberts.

CHAPTER 14

LET ME PRAY FOR YOU

Right now, I want you to focus on God. Let me tell you that although I'm not physically standing in front of you, I believe there is no distance in prayer. Concentrate on these words — God is the Source of my total supply. Close out everything from your physical eyes and see God with your spiritual eyes. See God as <u>more</u> than able to supply exceedingly, abundantly above anything you could ask or think.

See God as your Source physically.

See God as your Source financially.

See God as your Source spiritually.

THE SOURCE OF YOUR TOTAL SUPPLY.

Remember *Philippians 4:19* says, *"My God <u>shall</u> supply <u>all</u> your need according to his riches in glory* *by Christ Jesus."* You and I are not to look to each other, but only look to God as the Source of supply.

Right now, let your spiritual eyes focus on God Himself Who said, *"I am the Lord that healeth thee" (Exodus 15:26)*, and be expecting, expecting, expecting — I mean be in an attitude and atmosphere of <u>expectation</u> of the <u>miraculous</u> from the hand of God.

See God as your Source of total supply. See Him in Heaven, waiting to release the angels in your behalf as you stretch forth with the full force of your faith and <u>expect</u> and <u>expect</u> a miracle in Jesus' Name.

LET ME PRAY FOR YOU ... NOW!

Even if I can't see you with my eyes or touch you with my hands, and you can't see me or feel me touching you in prayer, we both have reached the point where our spirit can SEE GOD AS OUR SOURCE. We're looking up to God Himself Who said, *"I am the Lord who healeth thee" (Exodus 15:26)*.

I want you to be in a <u>spirit of prayer</u>, your very soul on fire with the tremendous reality of God being your Source of total supply . . . this very instant . . . and tomorrow . . . and all your tomorrows. As I start praying for you, the important thing is to FOCUS ON GOD — not on me, but straight on God. I'm ready. Now start focusing your faith on God and start expecting to receive back from Him according to your need.

"Satan, I come against you in the Name of Jesus Christ of Nazareth! You foul, tormenting sickness . . . disease . . . need . . . oppression. You come out! Come out! Go . . . and never come back! Thank God, our Source, Who heals us. Amen and amen.

"God, I come to You in the Name of Jesus Christ of Nazareth for Your mighty healing and delivering power to miraculously flow with this my friend who is focusing their faith directly on You now.

"Heavenly Father, I take Jesus as my personal Lord and Savior. I repent of every sin and I turn my back on it right now. I ask You to cleanse me, forgive me and give me a brand-new start. I believe Jesus died on the cross, was buried and on the third day was resurrected, and because He lives I can have eternal life. Thank You, Father, in Jesus' Name. Amen and amen."

Now let's lift our hearts and our hands and praise the Lord.

Let's say it out loud together:

"GOD, YOU ARE A GOOD GOD! AND YOU ARE ALWAYS A GOOD GOD!

"We worship and praise Your Name and expect our miracles, one by one, until ALL our needs are met. We give You the honor, the praise and the glory.

"From this moment, we are looking to You as our Source for the FULL MANIFESTATION of those miracles of deliverance. We believe our miracles are coming toward us every moment, and we reach out and receive them by faith. We will not let our miracles pass us by.

"Thank You, Lord. You are our God, our Source of total supply and we EXPECT OUR MIRACLES! In Jesus' Name, Amen and amen."

I urge you to pray this prayer <u>over</u> and <u>over</u> until it <u>gets in your spirit, your inner man</u>. I don't know how many times it will take — maybe one, two, a dozen times, or even more. The important thing is to get it inside you until you feel it, and know it, and can send your faith to God without hesitation, discouragement or any other hindrance.

I encourage you to pray this prayer like this, but don't stop with it. Watch for your own prayer to form by the Holy Spirit within you and open your lips to God. Watch, also, for that important moment when you know God is **YOUR** Source . . . with no ifs, ands, or maybe-sos.

I have great faith that as you read this book all the way through enough times, and pray this prayer until it has gotten into your spirit, as well as felt your own prayer formed by the Holy Spirit in you, **THAT YOU'LL NEVER BE THE SAME PERSON AGAIN.**

Continue to repeat: "I will not be defeated. My 'due season' will come. I will receive a miracle, then another, until I am a miracle person, **ALIVE AND ON FIRE WITH MY FAITH THAT GOD IS BOTH A GOOD GOD . . . AND . . . MY SOURCE OF TOTAL SUPPLY.**"

God bless you — and He does — and I believe He will!

And remember: You can reach our ABUNDANT LIFE PRAYER GROUP, 24 hours a day, 7 days a week.

Call (918) 495-7777

or you can reach me, or Richard, by writing:

Oral or Richard Roberts
Tulsa, Oklahoma 74171

Our Seed-Faith Gift to You!

Select any one or two of these books by Oral or Evelyn or Richard or Lindsay as our gift. This is our seed into your life — free and postage paid.

☐ **A Daily Guide to Miracles**
  by Oral Roberts   LC 101

☐ **The Roberts Family Guide to Miracles**
  by Oral, Evelyn, Richard and Lindsay Roberts   LC 226

☐ **A Prayer Cover Over Your Life**
  by Oral Roberts   LC 195

☐ **It's Time to Get Out of Debt Supernaturally**
  by Oral Roberts   LC 381

☐ **Miracle of Seed-Faith**
  by Oral Roberts   LC 105

☐ **Three Most Important Steps to Your Better Health and Miracle Living**
  by Oral Roberts   LC 112

☐ **You Can Be Blessed Not Stressed**
  by Richard and Lindsay Roberts   LC 284

(Seed-Faith gift request form continues on next page.)

❑ **He's the God of a Second Chance**
by Richard Roberts
LC 111

❑ **How You Can Touch Heaven With Your Faith**
by Richard Roberts
LC 258

❑ **How You Can Be Free From the Pain of Guilt**
by Richard Roberts
LC 414

❑ **Whither Thou Goest**
by Evelyn Roberts
LC 171

❑ **Coping With Grief**
by Evelyn Roberts
ENC 074

❑ **36 Hours With An Angel**
by Lindsay Roberts
LC 233

❑ Yes, I would like to receive one year's free subscription to *Abundant Life* magazine.

❑ Yes, I would like to receive one year's subscription to *Daily Blessing*. Enclosed is $2 or more.   784

❑ Yes, I would like to help you continue God's work through the Oral Roberts Ministries. Here is my $_____ Seed-Faith gift to carry on the work God has called you to do.

*Name*_____
*Address*_____
*City*_____
*State*_____ *ZIP*_____

Fill out and mail to: **Oral Roberts, Tulsa, OK 74171**

I care about you!

I want to invite you to write me. When you tell me what you're going through, I can know better how to write you back . . . and how to pray and help you believe God for A FLOW OF ABUNDANT MIRACLES to flood your life. *Simply fill out the Prayer Sheet* or address your personal letter to:

Oral Roberts
Tulsa, Oklahoma 74171

In Canada write:
Oral Roberts
Toronto, Ontario M4P 2G2

And when you write, I encourage you to consider planting a seed of your faith to God through this ministry. It's one of the best ways I know to help you release your faith to God and to look to Him alone to supply all your need according to Philippians 4:19.

PRAYER SHEET

Please pray for the needs I've written below.

_____

_____

_____

_____

_____

_____

_____

_____

_____

_____

Signature

I would like to plant this Seed-Faith gift of
$_____, believing for God to multiply it
back to me in a miracle harvest (Luke 6:38)!

NAME _____

ADDRESS _____

CITY _____

STATE _____ **ZIP** _____

785

Are you hurting?

**PRAYER TOWER,
ORAL ROBERTS
UNIVERSITY**

A prayer partner wants to reach out in love and concern to help you. We're here 24 hours a day, 7 days a week to put a Prayer Cover over you for your miracle.

This very moment a prayer partner is waiting for your call.

CALL:
(918) 495-7777

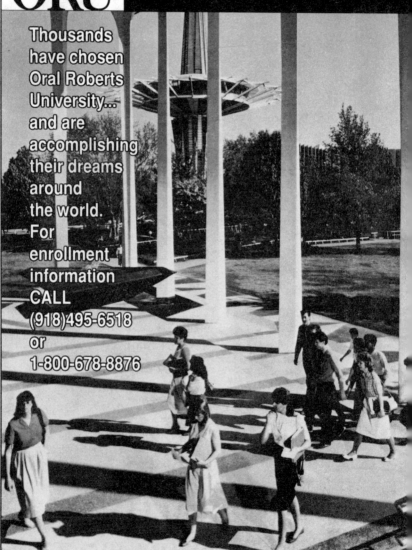